30 ARGUMENTS AGAINST THE EXISTENCE OF "GOD"

HEAVEN, HELL, SATAN, AND DIVINE DESIGN,

JONATHAN MS PEARCE

FOREWORD BY
DAN BARKER

30 Arguments Against the Existence of "God", Heaven, Hell, Satan, and Divine Design

Cover design: Jules Bailey and Onus Books

Trade paperback ISBN: 978-1-8382391-2-1

OB 19/34

Praise for this volume:

Alvin Plantinga talks of two dozen (or so) arguments. Rebecca Goldstein speaks of 36. Jonathan Pearce writes on 30. I could reduce the arguments down to five, or three, or one. The one is the *Outsider Test for Faith* highlighted by Pearce, which Richard Carrier says is "one of the most effective and powerful arguments for atheism", while James Lindsay calls it a "silver-bullet argument." Two makes three with the lack of objective evidence for biblical miracles, and the problem of horrendous suffering. Three then five with how the Bible debunks itself, and especially science (evolution, biblical archeology, and free will).

But since believers aren't usually reasoned out of a faith that they were never reasoned into, the prolific Pearce expertly throws the book at them. I'm a fan of his. Highly recommended reading!

– John W. Loftus, philosopher and counter-apologist with 12 books, including *The Case against Miracles* and *God and Horrendous Suffering.*

A concise but very philosophically sophisticated presentation of thirty evergreen problems for both theism in general and Abrahamic religions specifically. A must for the bookshelves of both atheists (to quickly reference powerful arguments) and theists (to understand the strongest and most commonly-used points of their opposition).

– Gunther Laird, author of *The Unnecessary Science: A Critical Analysis of Natural Law Theory*

Philosophical arguments for and against the existence of a deity abound, not only in academic circles, but also in the volatile arena of social media. For those wishing to wade into the controversy, the idea of acquainting oneself with the wide variety of philosophical and theological arguments can be rather daunting. Pearce's *30 Arguments Against the Existence of "God"* provides the reader with just such an introduction. With a down-to-earth and humorous tone, Pearce walks the reader through many of these confusing and complicated philosophical topics. If you are interested in breaking into the discussion on the existence of God, this is the book for you.

– Dr Joshua Bowen, author of *The Atheist Handbook to the Old Testament, Volume 1*

Why would a perfect god create anything at all in the first place?
Why does God love abortion so much when his followers hate it?
Has the theistic moral compass gone completely haywire?
From the God of the gaps to the Devil in the details, Jonathan Pearce asks—and answers—all the deep questions, closes the loopholes and escape clauses Yahweh uses to wiggle out of tight spots, and demonstrates without a doubt how the plan of salvation makes no damn sense and the Christian God is a tool (in every sense of the word). The perfect gift for every believing friend and frenemy in your life.

– David Fitzgerald, author of *Nailed, Jesus: Mything in Action* and *The Complete Heretic's Guide to Western Religion* series.

Jonathan Pearce has written an outstanding book in which key philosophical arguments against the existence of "God" are presented in clear, easily accessible chapters. I found the book compelling and thought-provoking. Written in Pearce's usual style of distilling philosophy down to clear prose, this book will allow any educated person to understand and appreciate the logic behind these arguments. Since I am a biologist rather than a philosopher, I quite appreciated the fact that I did not get distracted by terms and reasoning that might be more suited to the professional philosopher.

While the entire book holds together under a unifying theme, the 30 arguments can easily be consumed in small packets. Once I started the book, I was unable to put it down, and each of the chapters is so intellectually stimulating that I found myself stopping frequently to contemplate the implications of the reasoning. One can read a few chapters and then take some time to think about them.... A reader can pick up the book, turn to any chapter, and enjoy the mental stimulation.

This is an excellent book for those who want a clear philosophical basis for rejecting the idea of an all-knowing, all-loving, all-powerful god. In my years as a university teacher, I have witnessed many young people questioning the world view with which they were raised. This book would be the perfect place from which to start this complex but fascinating journey.

– Dr Joseph Berger, author of *Science and Spirituality: An Introduction for Students, Secular People & the Generally Curious*

Jonathan MS Pearce is a talented writer with a thoroughly enjoyable conversational style. While I tend to abhor philosophy, this little book provides a very nice, easy-to-read and comprehensive overview of a number of key philosophical issues pertaining to topics of God, religion and theology. This is an essential read for anyone with an interest in the viability of faith, whether it be theirs or another.

– Dr Kipp Davis, author of *Gleanings from the Caves* and *Dead Sea Scrolls Fragments in the Museum Collection*

Look no further for the strongest arguments against God! This book really takes the bloviation of philosophy and packages it for all to understand. Most theists want to start with philosophical arguments rather than the theological ones because of the absurd ideas presented by their tradition. However, Pearce encourages this and cuts the tree down at its roots: No rotten apples to eat from after reading this book. I have had the opportunity to watch him use these arguments in debate format with much success. Pearce has an addictive writing style that gets to the bottom of the age-old questions sparking endless debate on the OmniGod issue.

– Derek Lambert, host of *Mythvision Podcast*

Acknowledgements

This book was a blast to write – I just love talking about these sorts of arguments. But you can't complete any project on simple enjoyment alone. With this one, as with other previous works, I am indebted to Dana Horton, Jörg Fehlmann, and Geoff Benson for their time and awesome proofing. Finally, a special thanks as well to long-term supporter Lex Lata, whose eagle eyes were very welcome and highly valued. Wonderful people, they are. Honestly, I cannot thank them enough.

Jules Bailey's contribution to the cover design was almost divine. You know, divine design… Except, this cover won't give you cancer or instigate a tsunami.

Of course, the great Dan Barker deserves a huge proportion of gratitude, served with a healthy dollop of respect. He's such an accomplished man, but, more than that, he's a great human being who works tirelessly for the cause.

I must also thank all of my blog and now column readers, readers whom I have used as philosophical guinea pigs. Well, I see it as slightly more humane than that. I truly appreciate their continued support.

About the Author

Jonathan MS Pearce is a former teacher and author from Hampshire, UK, who has dedicated many years to studying all manner of things philosophical and theological. A philosopher with a marked interest in religion, he became a founder member of the *Skeptic Ink Network* (SIN) before moving to write for *Patheos Nonreligious* (Pearce's blog is *A Tippling Philosopher*). More recently, he has become a columnist and feature writer for *OnlySky*, where he hopes to impact the world positively with all of the wonderful contributors there. The site is a media platform tailored to a nonreligious and religiously unaffiliated audience, hoping to give them greater voice and representation. He also has an active *YouTube* channel (*A Tippling Philosopher*) and asks that you drop by for some talking-head thoughts.

As a founder member of the Tippling Philosophers, from which his blog and channel titles originated, a friendly group of disparate believers, non-believers, and sort-of believers, based in Hampshire, he is a big advocate of casual philosophy groups meeting over pints of good ale. He lives with his partner and twin boys and wonders how she puts up with him. Being diagnosed with primary progressive multiple sclerosis, he would like to personally thank God for that gift, though rely more reasonably on science to find a treatment (which he did do, with successful stem cell therapy that has kept him stable for a couple of years – a resurrection of sorts but certainly not a miracle).

Other books by Jonathan MS Pearce:

Free Will? An Investigation into Whether We Have Free Will Or Whether I Was Always Going to Write This Book

The Little Book of Unholy Questions

The Nativity: A Critical Examination

Beyond An Absence of Faith: Stories About the Loss of Faith and the Discovery of Self

13 Reasons to Doubt (ed.)

The Problem with "God": Classical Theism under the Spotlight

Did God Create the Universe from Nothing? Countering William Lane Craig's Kalam Cosmological Argument

Filling the Void: A Selection of Humanist and Atheist Poetry

Not Seeing God: Atheism in the 21st Century (ed.)

The Resurrection: A Critical Examination of the Easter Story

Why I Am Atheist and Not a Theist: How To Do Knowledge, Meaning, and Morality in a Godless World

As Johnny Pearce:

Twins: A Survival Guide for Dads

Survival of the Fittest: Metamorphosis

Survival of the Fittest: Adaptation

The Curse of the Maya

To Bert Bigelow.
Thanks for accompanying me
on this journey,
benign Pied Pipers
singing songs of a better place.

CONTENTS

Foreword

By Dan Barker

When I was doing the research for my book *Free Will Explained*, I came across Jonathan Pearce's excellent book *Free Will?* I was impressed not only with the content, but with the writing, which made me determined to pull a quote from his book to make mine look better. I had no choice. Jonathan has a sharp mind and an engaging style. He is a true philosopher. You can see that I used to be merely a preacher because my title is emphatic while his ends with a judicious question mark. However, as much as I appreciate his writing, we do have disagreements. Jonathan thinks God has a judgemental behaviour, but he is wrong about that. God has a judgmental behavior. In the first chapter of *30 Arguments against the Existence of God*, he talks about "analysing reality" when he should really be "analyzing reality," which is what we smart Americans know how to do. (See: we also know to put the comma inside the quote marks—or should I say "inside the inverted commas"?—for some superior reason.) Perhaps he will acknowledge his errors in the Acknowledgments, I mean Acknowledgements.

Other than that, we are in complete agreement. OmniGod (as Jonathan calls him) not only *does* not exist—he *cannot* exist. Arguing for the existence of a being whose properties are mutually exclusive is like arguing for the existence of a married bachelor. Perhaps a lesser god exists—one who can be defined coherently—but the traditional Abrahamic God is an impossibility.

I used to believe in that impossible God. I was "born again," accepting Christ as my Lord and Savior (or Saviour). While worshipping my master, I felt the joy of his presence and sometimes got goosebumps as I was singing hymns to his glory. I often saw what

1

looked like answers to my prayers. When I was an enthusiastic teenager, I accepted what I was convinced was a calling from God to the ministry and spent nineteen years preaching the Good News that we can escape the fierce wrath of the loving God by accepting the bloody sacrifice of his blameless biological son on the cross thereby escaping the torture of hell and gaining a blissful eternal life in heaven after the Second Coming of Jesus, which could be tonight. I was an associate pastor in three California churches, a missionary to Mexico for a total of almost two years, a cross-country traveling evangelist for eight years, and a Christian songwriter. (I am still receiving royalties from that music.) In the Foreword to my book *Godless*, Richard Dawkins says I was not just a preacher: I was the kind of preacher you would not want to sit next to on a bus.[1]

Then I changed my mind. After a grueling four to five-year process of re-evaluation, I became an atheist in mid-1983 and formally left the ministry in January 1984. People give different reasons for why they leave religion and become atheists or agnostics. (See the testimonies of other now-nonbelieving ministers and priests in The Clergy Project.[2]) For me, it was initially and primarily the bible. I still strongly recommend, as I used to do in the ministry, that people read the bible. Read it carefully and completely. It will do wonders for your education. When I read the scriptures with an open mind instead of a worshipful attitude, I realized (realised) that the "God of love" I believed in simply does not exist. This fact does not necessarily lead to atheism (because the nonexistence of the biblical god does not mean other gods do not exist), but it does demolish the worship of such a god. And when you stop worshipping you can start thinking.

After leaving the ministry and beginning to speak publicly about my atheism, I have had to move beyond bible criticism into philosophy and science. Since 1985, I have done 137 public debates with theists, and by the time you read this it will be more than 140. These are formal

---

[1] Barker, Dan (2008), *Godless: How an Evangelical Preacher Became One of America's Leading Atheists*, Berkeley: Ulysses Press.
[2] See *The Clergy Project*, https://clergyproject.org/ (12/06/2021, or as Jonathan would say, 06/12/2021…)

moderated timed debates in front of an audience, many at universities (such as Oxford and Harvard), and many in churches. Additionally, I have done hundreds of informal debates on the radio, television and (especially since the pandemic) by remote video. I am not the best debater in the world, but if there *are* any powerful arguments for the existence of God, by now I should have heard them.

That alone should be enough reason to reject theism, but it gets better. Not only are there no good arguments *for* a god, which are dealt with by rebuttal, there are many good arguments *against* a god, which require their own rebuttal if faith is to be maintained. In *30 Arguments against the Existence of God*, Jonathan Pearce puts the shoe on the other foot. He makes a positive case *against* theism.

In Chapter 8, Jonathan gives one of my favorite examples. I call it FANG: the Freewill Argument for the Nonexistence of God. Simply put, if you know the future you can't have free will. You may or may not think humans have free will (depending on your theology or philosophy), but if you believe in God, you certainly think *he* has free will. However you define it, free will requires options, and if you know the future, you have no options: the future is fixed, leaving you with nothing to choose. (This also puts limits on God's power, but that is a different argument.) If you are omniscient, you are not an autonomous person—you are a slave or a robot executing software. Some apologists try to wriggle out of this by claiming that God exists outside of time, but that just replaces one incoherency with another. If an all-knowing trinitarian deity exists, it is not "God in three persons," as the hymn proclaims,[1] but "God in three incoherencies."

"OmniGod is a collection of properties and characteristics that just don't get on well with each other, fighting like ferrets in a bag," Jonathan writes. Yes, and the ferrets end up devouring each other—like matter and antimatter—leaving nothing but an empty bag.

---

[1] "Holy, Holy, Holy" (1826) by Reginald Heber contains the words, "God in three persons. Blessed Trinity."

If you are like me—if you *love* these juicy morsels of thought—then you will relish the marvelous banquet Jonathan Pearce has prepared in the following pages. (I guess I should write "marvellous banquet.") I used to preach about the need to nourish the soul, but I now encourage you to nourish your mind. Scan Jonathan's tempting menu to see what you might sample: "The Soul Doesn't Exist," or "The Problem of Evil," or "Infinite Punishment for Finite Crimes," or "The Bible Is Not a Good Source of Morality," or "Where is God Hiding?" Go ahead and choose—even if you don't think you have free will—and you will "taste and see" that the Lord is not good[1] and that therefore rejecting the OmniGod is not a loss of anything at all. The freedom to think for yourself makes life so much more delicious.

---

[1] Psalm 34:8. "Taste and see that the Lord is good."

Introduction

By Jonathan MS Pearce

There are as many versions of God as there are believers. Indeed, many versions of God are perfect versions of those believers themselves! We are nothing if not good at projecting, we humans. Because there are so many iterations of this entity called God, it is necessary for me to select one of them, and go with it. This is what I did in *The Problem with "God": Classical Theism Under the Spotlight*. I put God in inverted commas to become "God" in order to hint at the idea that there is a problem with settling on one particular understanding of God. I continue that theme here.

So my version of God – the one that I have in the crosshairs in this book – needs to be one that most people would understand. After all, I'm not going to pick a fight with a bizarre manifestation of God that virtually no one ascribes to. That would be pointless. No, I want to pick the most common version, one that at least shares common traits with most other versions if not fully reflecting their range of nuances.

This divine form is the God of "classical theism": something I like to call *OmniGod*. That is to say, this god is omnipotent (all-powerful), omniscient (all-knowledgeable), and omnibenevolent (all-loving). I will add to this, as part of omniscience, the idea of full divine foreknowledge, such that God knows all future events that will, or hypothetically could, come to pass. There are a number of other attributes that others may and often do add to this list (such as omnipresent and eternal) but I will stick mainly to these.

Thus God isn't just some super-cool hammer-wielding superhuman (for example), but a far more abstract affair. As God from biblical times was beaten back by the early lamps of enlightenment,

5

retreating in the face of a more accurate understanding of how the world works, God became more abstract: From living amongst us to retreating behind the mountains, from living outside of our region to living in the skies above, from living outside of our solar system to living beyond the physical reality of our universe. God has lost his, her, or its body to become an idea – a concept – with perfect or maximal abilities.

God is now a faceless, bodiless, capeless, hammerless, underpants-over-leotardless superhero.

Of course, he never used to be. I say "he" here because I really do mean "he". In an abstract sense and form, God has no sex or gender. God is without body and human anthropomorphic traits. But if we take the god of the Abrahamic faiths (of Christianity, Islam, and Judaism), then God definitely *did* have a body. For this, I advise the reader to circle back to…the Bible. But if that's too much of an effort, you could read Professor Francesca Stavrakopoulou's magisterial book *God: An Anatomy*. God originally had a body, existed within a pantheon, and even had a consort.

It might be worth noting here that the Hebrew Bible – and the first five books thereof (known as the Torah in Judaism and the Pentateuch in Christianity) – had multiple sources. This is something that almost all modern Hebrew Bible scholars now agree on. Within these sources, there are different conceptions of Yahweh – the Old Testament/Hebrew Bible iteration of the Judeo-Christian God. One source shows Yahweh to be pretty darned strong and knowledgeable – but not really *omni*potent or *omni*scient. Just better or more so than all the other gods (who equally existed in the pantheon). A slightly later source (the "P" or "Priestly" source) saw Yahweh somewhat closer to the version we now understand.

Indeed, one way to distinguish the earlier source(s) from the "Priestly" source is in the anthropomorphic way that God is depicted: he walks, he builds from the dirt, he has gaps in knowledge, he interacts physically with people, and so on.

Time hasn't so much ravaged God's body as philosophically eliminated it. And, along with it, any such bodily interpretations found in the Hebrew Bible upon which those three faiths were founded.

As God has become more abstract, his characteristics have become more obvious, and stridently claimed. It has been a result of a school playground argument.

"My god's better than yours: he's a storm god and could beat yours in a fight."

Which eventually evolves to something like this:

"No, my god's better than yours because he is the only one. Yours doesn't even exist. And my god, God, is not just powerful, he's omnipotent. And omniscient. And omnibenevolent. And probably omnipresent. Oh, and infinite."

"Yeah, but…infinity plus one?"

So several thousand years later, we get a thoroughly refined abstract God that looks nothing like the one found in the pages of the Hebrew Bible, but that is still supposed to be that god. And this is why theologians exist – their impossible job is to square this most circular of circles.

It's all nonsense, of course. You can't square that circle in a reality where neither squares nor circles exist. (Just for the sake of analogy clarity, squares and circles *do* exist in our reality, but arguably as merely concepts in our minds. Just like God, really.)[1]

OmniGod it is then. This is the term I will use to refer to an omnipotent, omniscient, omnibenevolent god with full divine foreknowledge. I will call this particular incarnation of a god, for sake of simplicity, "God" (as well as OmniGod).

There are – and this book is entirely concerned with this – problems with defining or understanding these omni-characteristics.

---

[1] For understanding of the conceptualism of ideas like this – because it is crucial for my worldview as a humanist and atheist – see my book *Why I Am Atheist and Not a Theist: How To Do Knowledge, Meaning, and Morality in a Godless World* (Pearce 2021).

Dan Barker (atheist activist, author, and debater) grapples with these characteristics in his book *Godless*, here musing about omniscience:[1]

> If there is a God, maybe he could accomplish this relatively simple (to him) task of keeping track of the universe by existing somehow "outside" the universe in an unimaginably huge dimension, looking "down" (or "across" or "into") our cosmos. (This hypothesis seems to have coherency problems of its own, which I deal with elsewhere.) But that is not the problem. The problem is God himself. In order for God to know everything, he has to know not only about all the unknown galaxies and extrasolar planetary systems and where all the undiscovered diamond mines and my missing socks are located, he also has to know everything about himself. He has to know what he is going to think next. He has to anticipate that he is going to need to know what he is going to think next, and after that into the infinite future. Like the computer virus, an omniscient God gets caught in an infinite loop keeping track of itself and cannot have a single thought. (Maybe that's why the God of the Old Testament blows his stack so much.) It doesn't matter what method God uses to store and retrieve data in his super mind, he has to have some kind of internal representation. If theists argue that the intelligence of God is something altogether different from human or computer intelligence, then they are admitting that the idea of omniscience is meaningless. If "all-knowing" does not compare with "knowing," then the phrase lacks relevance to human understanding and we may as well say that "God is mmpfghrmpf" instead of "God is omniscient."

> Some theologians admit these and other problems and tinker with the definition of omniscience. Some, such as Greg Boyd, claim that God has a "limited omniscience," that he knows everything that is knowable but that not everything is knowable, not even to God. Others suggest that "all-knowing" means "knowing more than anyone else" or "super

---

[1] Barker, Dan (2008), *Godless*, Berkeley, CA: Ulysses Press, p. 123-24.

knowing." Maybe God knows soooo much more than we do that it amounts to the same thing. Fair enough, but this underscores the fact that omniscience–total omniscience–is incoherent. Perhaps a lesser god exists, but a god who is truly omniscient cannot exist. It therefore does not exist.

A further important note to make is that this book will primarily be aimed at the Christian god, because that is the context in which I usually operate, but it doesn't need to be. Effectively, this god is the god of Judaism and of Islam too, even if you do have to squint and cock your head sideways sometimes to see this (and forget half of your holy book).

At the times where I do end up using Christian references – say Doubting Thomas and his unfair access to greater evidence – the reader should be able to tweak the example a little to make it fit with their context. For example, Thomas could become Muhammad or one of his close accomplices, Moses or Aaron, or any other favoured Hebrew Bible player with preferential access to God and evidence for God. Or whatever character fits the mould in whatever religion you are analysing.

As an aside, I apologise to those almost certainly rare readers who have read my previous work as some of the arguments within this collection have appeared in previous books and online articles in one form or another. When you have written over a dozen books on the subject, and over 3,500 online articles, this becomes an inevitability. Hopefully, this collection of arguments is a useful reminder for those who have read them before, and (like me) tend to forget them within the week. These previously utilised arguments have predominantly been reformulated and remoulded for this anthology. That said, there are plenty of new and shiny ones to get your teeth into, as well as additions and editions to those others.

Anyway, that's enough preamble, let's get on with it. I'll be starting big and narrowing it down, from pervasive existential ideas down to biblical minutiae.

Final point: I'm going to try really hard to call God "it" because, from a philosophical point of view, that is the pronoun that makes most rational sense to use. "It" sounds odd, but that is because we are so used to reading God as an inferred male. Anywho, "it" it is, isn't it?

Who knew that smashing God would also smash the patriarchy? Or something.

Part One

BEING, DESIGN, AND CREATION

Ontology is the study of existence, being, becoming, and reality. As such, it is pertinent to discussions concerning God's existence.

When we look at God's existence, of course we need to consider its characteristics. God's characteristics are *necessary* for the theologian because God is, for them, a *necessary* being. Which means, according to the theologian, that if you are to imagine any possible world, God would exist in each and every one. I won't get into the details of this, and whether "possible worlds" even holds as a philosophical concept or method of analysing reality. But it is interesting that believers may be faced with issues about how God might not be able to change its characteristics. Those "omnis" are set in abstract stone such that God is *immutable*. We will return to this idea in due course.

Or, we could say, if God is necessary, then God's characteristics are necessary. One of the potential corollaries of this is that the world – this world (or, indeed, any world) – might well be *equally* necessary. If God is necessary, and its characteristics are necessary, and God exists outside of time and yet "causally prior" to creation, then any creation is a necessary extension of God's existence. Ergo, any world created "whilst" God is in that timeless state is as ontologically necessary as God. Which is to say that you or I, that chair over there, and that virus over here, are all as equally necessary as God, being instantaneous outpourings at the point of creation. In a sense, there is no "time", no "instant", where God exists without the created entities that it

11

supposedly brought into being. There is no sense of contingent because if God exists, that which it creates exists equally necessarily.

If God has these necessary attributes, and what is created is defined by these attributes, then you could argue that if God exists in every possible world you can think of, so do we. Again, this is something to which we will return.

God is, for most believers, perfect. The subject area that involves rumination on this is called "Perfect Being Theology" (PBT). PBT proponents seek to set out what such perfection must look like as manifested in God and God's actions.

This sounds intuitively plausible: "Hey, God is perfect!"

But even that I struggle to comprehend adequately.

I can only understand *perfect* as a goal-directed adjective such that A is perfect *for* B. Or this catapult is perfect *for* getting this stone over the wall in such and such a manner. Perfection is understood in terms of functionality or instrumentality. When we use one thing in order to do or achieve another thing, it can be perfect for the job. There is also perhaps a subjective element to this.

Now, one could say that God is *perfect* at *being* God, but this implies a circularity. What does it really mean to say that God is perfect? Is it perfect at getting a stone over the wall? Perfect at being loving, merciful and just, at designing, and being moral? Is God perfect at being perfect? How can we make sense of this?

Even looking at some kind of intrinsic notion of perfection is problematic. For instance, establishing what a perfect painting is, is an entirely subjective process, depending upon personal tastes. And this applies to all sorts of things such that perfection becomes either subjective or incoherent. Being perfectly powerful and knowledgeable are admittedly simpler proficiencies to hold, conceptually.

Another problem is that perfection of a being involves multiple aspects. As the classic problem goes, God cannot be perfectly just *and* perfectly merciful since to be perfectly just assumes punishing justly for a misdemeanour, and to be perfectly merciful assumes some kind of leniency. More on this in a later argument.

With all of these characteristics in conflict, the theist retreats to *maximal* perfection, a sort of optimal scenario given all of the nuances and variables. But this becomes arbitrary and subjective. One more ounce of mercy and one less ounce of justice might be perfect for a God wanting to achieve A, but vice versa might be better for wanting to achieve B.

Therefore, we need to establish, without circularity (that might confer no meaning at all, such that "God is God") or incoherence, what God is to be perfect *for*. And we need to do this before establishing whether God is or even can be perfect. To have a timeless God sitting there and label it as perfect is, to me, meaningless. At that single moment, causally prior to creation, it is hard to describe God as anything other than potential.

Therefore, given the subjective nature of appraisals of perfection, and given the functionality of the term, I see any argument or claim about God that uses the term perfection without clarity of explaining the goal as incoherent.

Parking this, let us consider that first manifestation of God and whether it would even create anything at all.

1 – Why Would God Create at All?

This is one of those arguments that I have often used in one form or another in my previous work. It is important, though, because it cuts right to the heart of everything – or anything – in existence.

The question we perhaps need to ask of God is why did it create anything at all? I mean, really, why? What is the point? What is the point of us? Of the universe, including black holes and tsunamis, malaria and debilitating mental health? Humans are left – at least, those still clinging onto belief in a supposedly supreme being – trying to desperately work out what the answers to these questions might be without even the slightest peep out of the creator itself. Indeed, God appears to have been on holiday for 2,000 years and has disconnected the phone.

Why indeed. We can but guess.

The problem – and, for this, return to previous ideas of a necessary, immutable, perfect God – is the idea that God is, indeed, perfect. Okay, that might make no sense, but let's grant the theist at least this much for the sake of the argument. I like the idea that they might be "hoist by their own petard".[1] Something that is sheer perfection will not be lacking anything. And some entity not lacking anything will not have a need for anything. No lacking, no needs, no desires.

If God exists, causally prior to creation, in some scenario of perfection, then there is no rationale for God "deciding" to create

---

[1] Fun fact: the phrase's meaning is literally that a bomb-maker is lifted ("hoist") off the ground with his own bomb (a "petard" is a small explosive device).

anything. Simply put, OmniGod wouldn't create because creation would invalidate its omni-characteristics and ideas of perfection.

This can be formulated into a syllogism:

(1) If the Christian God exists, then GodWorld is the unique best possible world.

(2) If GodWorld is the unique best possible world, then the Christian God would maintain GodWorld.

(3) GodWorld is false because the Universe (or any non-God object) exists.

(4) Conclusion: Therefore, the Christian God, as so defined, does not exist.

Let me explain this a little. An omniscient being would be aware of the fact of itself existing alone for eternity as GodWorld is the unique best possible world that could ever exist. And because such a god is essentially morally perfect, it would not have a motivating reason to intentionally alter the overall maximal purity (and quality) of the unique best possible world. Further, any alteration in overall purity by the introduction of a universe or any Non-God object would, by necessity, be a *degradation* of overall purity and, therefore, overall quality. Thus, God would not logically introduce limited entities (i.e., humans) into GodWorld, each with their own unimpressive set of degraded great-making properties.[1] But this is what the creation myths of Genesis (as particular religious examples) record. Whilst Adam and Eve clearly do have a few great-making properties (knowledge, power), they have them to an unimpressive degree. So introducing such beings would result in a degradation of overall ontological purity and overall ontological quality. To suggest God is in the degrading business is to suggest it was not maximally great or perfect in the first place.

Part of the problem with considering what God would decide to do in GodWorld is that time would not yet exist. (Indeed, you *could*

---

[1] All the winning properties that make God so great, that we also appear to have a much smaller supply of.

make an argument that God wouldn't exist since what is existence absent interaction with any other entity?) Without the creation of spacetime – since time is a function or characteristic of a physical universe – you would not get time, and all the things that depend upon time. I don't see how ideas like "deciding" and "change" can happen without time.

Any time a theist is talking about God existing causally prior (because we can't even use the term "before" if we are devoid of time and a temporal framework) to the universe and deciding to do something, one presumes that God deliberated over the decision and variables, calculated the outcomes, and then reasoned on the back of them, and created GodWorld. Deliberating, calculating, and evaluating options are things involved in decision-making and require time. They also imply a of lack of knowledge. An entity that merely does what its nature programmes it to do is nothing more than a computer. We don't say a computer really "decides" things in the same way we understand human minds do.

The simple conclusion here is that there is no way that OmniGod would decide to create anything at all.

And yet here we are.

2 – God Is a Poor Designer

Let me start with some general philosophy before moving on to talk about particular instances of biological "design".

Let's put this design fault into a biblical context, with the understanding that this is aimed at the Abrahamic faiths. According to Genesis, God created Adam and Eve in a supposedly perfect scenario. They have been chosen to represent humanity in a big test (at least as has been understood and theologically developed over time): Not eating a fruit from the Tree of Knowledge. This presents a conundrum from the start: *Before* eating from a fruit that gives them the knowledge of *what is right and wrong*, they have to know that it is wrong to disobey God and eat some forbidden fruit. They are punished for making the *wrong* choice *before knowing what is wrong!*

Damn this logic game.

This is actually a fundamental flaw in the lucidity of the story. But, of course, this story was never an actual and real event that took place in history – this is obviously a myth. And myths don't need to make that much sense in the minutiae of their details.

Okay, let's allow that issue to slip and carry on with the story.

So, Adam and Eve represent humanity in this test. God knows in advance of this the result of the test, but it picks Adam and Eve to do it anyway. And it knows they are going to fail. God knows it has a glaring design flaw on his hands and yet still sets the test up. Further, if Adam and Eve are representative of humanity, then any human taking that test would have failed, and *we are all inherently faulty*. You, me, anyone and everyone we know – we would all have done the same thing as

17

Adam and Eve. This throws perfect design and creation down the proverbial drain.

If, however, Adam and Eve are not representative of humanity, then God has chosen non-representative people to take a test and fail. This is to say that had God ordered you, me, or other people that we know, not to eat from the tree, then there is every chance in this scenario that we would have followed orders. We would have passed the test. On account of this failure of a non-representative Adam and Eve, all other people, given the Fall and Original Sin as commonly understood, are punished.

It's bad enough to know we are being punished for the choice of Adam and Eve because we are all equally as shoddy as they are, but it's possibly worse to think we are being punished for the wrongdoing of this test when we could have passed the test ourselves!

Quite a two-horned dilemma.

God is either a poor designer or a moral monster.

Perhaps both.

The aforementioned Dan Barker also recognises this issue (as, indeed, many have):[1]

> The Christian God cannot be both omniscient and omnibenevolent. If God were omniscient, then he knew when he created Adam that Adam would sin. He *knew* human beings would suffer. Regardless of whether the existence of evil can be theologically explicated, an all-knowing Creator deliberately placed humans in its path. This is at least criminal negligence, if not malice. Those who invoke "free will" forget that we all act according to a human nature that was supposedly created by God himself. You can argue all around the bushes on this point, but you can't get away from the fact that Adam did not create his own nature. At the moment of creation, an omniscient deity would have been picturing the suffering and damnation of most of his creation. This is mean-spirited. God should have had an

---

[1] Barker, Dan (2008), *Godless*, Berkeley, CA: Ulysses Press, p. 124.

abortion rather than bring a child into such misery. Perhaps a lesser (or malevolent) god exists, but the problem of evil gives the lie to the claim that a god can be both all-good and all-powerful.

We humans appear to get punished for our sins quite a bit by OmniGod, according to theists. They believe in both earthly retribution (for example, floods caused by gays, as many more conservative theists believe) and afterlife retribution (fire and brimstone of hell, or simple annihilation of your soul). But one could argue that sinfulness has been hardwired into our DNA.

More on this in the next argument.

In the meantime, let me introduce you to some of the wonderful evolutionary design features of this world that we live in. There are countless examples. Hardcore theists will likely deny evolution. But even some moderate believers will extricate themselves from evolutionary problems by declaring they are *theistic evolutionists* – that God designed evolution as a way of creating the diversity of life. (Of course, this is not to ignore the many varieties of Christians who exist over the entire spectrum.)

Of course, in either case, God would still have full sovereignty and control over that which it has brought about. There must be some reason it wanted the *Acanthamoeba* (the parasite that can eat away at the human eye in a condition called *Acanthamoeba keratitis*) or the nematode *Onchocerca volvulus* (whose dead larval corpses in the human eye can cause blindness) to exist.

Let's read a little about the wonderful design of the latter, and our own body's design, that work together to cause river blindness:[1]

Unfortunately, the same cannot be said for the nematode *Onchocerca volvulus*, which causes an illness known as river blindness, or onchocerciasis. The worms are transmitted by

---

[1] Baggaley, Kate (2018), "Meet the menagerie of parasites that can live in human eyes", *Popular Science*, https://www.popsci.com/human-eye-parasites/ (retrieved 15/10/2021).

a kind of blackfly that breeds along moving water in parts of West Africa, Central and South America, and Yemen. A couple adult worms might not cause any noticeable symptoms. But if you are bitten over and over, you can end up with hundreds of thousands of their offspring moving through your skin in hopes of infecting the next fly to bite you, says Paul Cantey, a medical officer for onchocerciasis and scabies at the World Health Organization.

As with most eye parasites, the bulk of the damage is not caused by the worm itself but by our own immune system. When the larvae die, their corpses release bacteria that create proteins that trigger our body's inflammatory response. This can cause a number of skin problems, including intensely itchy spots and a loss of elastic tissue that leaves the skin fragile and prematurely wrinkled.

Meanwhile, if the larvae crawl onto the surface of your eye and die, your corneas can become inflamed. If left untreated, the cornea will eventually scar and cloud over, leading to vision loss and finally blindness. The worms can also blind people when they get inside the eye itself and die in the optic nerve.

The more larvae you have in your body, the greater the likelihood that some will unwittingly head to the eyes....

An estimated 198 million people live in areas where infected blackflies may transmit river blindness, Cantey says. At one time, there were villages in sub-Saharan Africa where 30 to 40 percent of the residents had lost their sight and people were forced to abandon millions of acres of arable land.

Which is nice.

There are many, many more graphic examples of this sort of design. But what needs to be remembered is that the theist has to explain each of these instances of design in the context of an all-loving god. God must either actively want these animals to exist as they are and has actively designed them so (if you deny evolution) or is not willing to step in and change things in the event of evolution throwing up such lifeforms.

In other words, God must have some reason or another for letting organisms exist that cause blindness, disability, suffering (to victims and their families), death, and so on, rather than lift a divine forefinger to do anything about them. God must want blindness, disability, and suffering to exist.

But there are more design issues.

Where *teleological* arguments concern themselves with how the universe looks as if it has been designed, or has meaning or purpose, *dysteleological* ones are a family of arguments that provide evidence that God does not exist because there are clear-cut examples of very poor design.

For the naturalist, there is no such thing as poor design in evolution. Simply put, there is no agency involved in evolution, and the process works in bringing things about using only pre-existing building blocks with no eye on the big picture. Evolution is only "interested in" (it has no agency and so is not really interested in anything – this is a turn of phrase to help explain) successfully getting an organism to reproductive age and to then reproduce.

The teleological argument for a designing God looks like this:

(1) Living things are too well-designed to have originated by chance.
(2) Therefore, life must have been created by an intelligent creator.
(3) This creator is God.

On the other hand, a dysteleological argument might run as follows:

(1) An omnipotent, omniscient, omnibenevolent creator God would create organisms that have optimal design.
(2) Organisms have features that are suboptimal.

21

(3) Therefore, God either did not create these organisms or is not omnipotent, omniscient, and omnibenevolent.

In the human body alone, bad design is rampant. Let me list some examples of poor design that simply wouldn't or shouldn't be the case in the event of OmniGod designing us:

- Women have narrow birth canals leading to painful births (almost akin to man-flu) and maternal deaths (okay, I feel bad about the last joke).
- Remaining with pregnancy, ectopic pregnancies, where a fertilised egg can implant into the fallopian tube, cervix, or ovary rather than the uterus, can cause huge problems too.
- Our digestive/alimentary canals share the same pathway as our breathing system. It would be better, as with other mammals like whales, if these were separate. Choking to death appears to be a design criterion for God. Thanks for that.
- Hernias (which used to cause intestinal blockage, gangrene and death) result from weaknesses in the abdominal wall caused by the development of the male testes.
- Wisdom teeth – poor quality, painful teeth.
- The appendix. These serve no present purpose and often get infected.
- Some muscles and nerves, left over from an evolutionary history, are barely or ever used. Other muscles have no use – such as ear moving muscles.
- The back is poorly "designed", with a host of problems, made worse because the spinal cord is unable to heal.
- The gene for synthesising our own vitamin C is defective (as it is with other primates), which can cause scurvy and death.

- Human (and many animal) eyes are poorly "designed" with an inverted retina that has caused many adaptations, resulting in blind spots.

You get the picture. And this is equally the case across all life forms. Evolution does just enough to allow the organism to continue living and pass on its genes to continue existing going forward. It doesn't start with a blank design slate and create, from scratch, the best possible way of functioning and achieving a given objective.

But seen in the light of OmniGod and all of its amazing design potential, these shortcomings make absolutely no sense at all.

Let me just emphasise that: the issues are fully explained given evolution under naturalism (life absent of supernatural forces like God). But they are not explicable in light of OmniGod. To explain these shortfalls, the theists, whether or not they deny evolution, have to do all sorts of crazy ad hoc rationalisations (create special arguments or explanations on the hoof) and tack them onto each example of bad design. The whole project is doomed as it makes the theist look silly, and God look even sillier.

Evolutionary theists have their work cut out too, because they still have to explain all these weird scenarios – especially the ones that involve pain and suffering – in light of a God who *could* do something about it but who *doesn't*.

3 – This Must Be a Perfect World

We have seen that if OmniGod exists, then there is no discernible reason why it might create at all. In addition, there is the idea that the creation it has produced is sub-optimal. However, it gets worse for the theist because we can apply this sort of argument to the universe as a whole – a universe that looks better designed for death and suffering than it does for life, what with its black holes and plate tectonics.

As I stated in my book *Why I am Atheist and Not a Theist*, a perfect creator, as God must be, would surely choose to create perfectly.

But we are here. Good old humans, on good old Earth, with its good old tsunamis and malaria, in this good old universe, with its good old supposed heat death, and good old life-sucking black holes. This universe is a perfect creation. Somehow, and at some point. It has to be, otherwise God is a sub-optimal creator. It has to be, otherwise God is creating unnecessary amounts of pain and suffering.

OmniGod cannot produce even one unit of unnecessary (gratuitous) pain or suffering. We can talk about 230,000 people dying in the 2004 tsunami, including any number of animals and ecosystems. But all that needs to happen to invalidate God's label of OmniGod (particularly omnibenevolence) is one stubbed toe and the related amount of gratuitous suffering.

So if this world is perfect, it has to have the perfect or optimal amount of suffering, in some manner.

But is it really? Is it *now*? Was it ever? Will it be perfect at some future point? The jury's out. Maybe we could be on a *journey* to perfection. Who knows…? I am just not sure that all the pain and suffering we see is *necessary* for that eventual perfection.

Let me explain. If life is not about present perfection but some journey to a future perfection, then we are concerning ourselves with moral consequentialism. In this moral framework, it is all about the ends, and the ends justify the means. In this case, the evil of pain and suffering is justified for the greater good of some perfect consequence.

To be more precise, the pain and suffering on this journey must be the perfect or optimal amount in order to obtain the end (whatever it is that God has in mind). It is not good enough just to say that we are on some journey towards perfection and this potential ending somehow excuses *any* amount of suffering on the way. We have to add that God *still* can't allow unnecessary pain and suffering.

Thus, any pain and suffering – whatever amount there *presently* is if you believe we are on a journey to a perfect end – is *absolutely necessary* in order to obtain that end. So 230,000 people *had* to die in that tsunami to achieve the proposed end. Luckily not 230,001, but also one less person could not die. 229,999 dying would somehow not allow the proposed end to come about. One less rat, one less bee, one less animal or plant of any description would have ruined the chance of the perfect outcome coming about.

So if we were theists, we would believe that this world is either perfect now (thus the present amount of suffering represents optimal perfection), *or* we are on the journey to a perfect world (thus the present amount of suffering represents the necessary optimal suffering needed for that eventual perfection).

Which is to say that if you stub your toe tomorrow, or if a baby gets cancer, or if another tsunami kills a further 230,000 people, those examples of suffering are *necessary*, and there cannot be one less unit of pain or suffering than there would or should be.

Whatever suffering the theist observes of the world around them, it must be necessarily perfect or optimal.

This is what famous philosopher Gottfried Liebniz admitted (who argued for the Ontological Argument, seeking to show that God was logically necessary). Polish philosopher Leszek Kolakowski summed up this theistic position excellently in the chapter in his book of the same name *Why Is There Something Rather Than Nothing?*:[1]

> Of course there is evil, sin and suffering in the world. Evil arises from the very imperfection of God's creatures; God could not have created them perfect, for then they would have been His equals, and it is logically impossible for there to be more than one God. God, Leibniz says - in accordance with traditional Christian theology - does not do evil, He merely allows it. But - and this is a crucial point - God allows only the minimum of evil that is possible in the world. God must be infinitely good because He is perfect, and goodness is entailed by perfection, by definition. He is also infinitely wise, and from those two attributes, goodness and wisdom, it follows that He must have created the best of all possible worlds - that is, a world in which the sum of good is as great as it could possibly be and the sum of evil as small as it could possibly be. God looked over all possible worlds and must have solved an infinitely complex equation which produced our world as the solution. A world with no evil in it may have been possible, but it would have to have been a world peopled by automata without free will; God calculated that our world, with all its evil and suffering, still produces infinitely more good than that other possible world without evil and without freedom. We live, therefore, in the best of all possible worlds, and this conclusion, which so infuriated Voltaire, follows ineluctably from the very concept of God as a perfect being. He is not only the Creator of everything but also the sovereign and loving father of His human subjects. We might wonder whether this argument could convince someone who is dying of hunger or being tortured to death, but the question does nothing to shake Liebniz's faith; he does not deny that evil and suffering exist, only that their existence is a good argument against God's goodness.

---

[1] Kolakowski, Leszek (2008), *Why Is There Something Rather Than Nothing?*, London: Penguin, p. 148-49.

Theodicy, the theory of divine justice, was for Liebniz (who coined the term) a subject of constant reflection.

One way or another, for the theist, this world is perfect, cancerous warts and all.

4 – God Loves Abortion!

If you are an avid reader of my other works (and, honestly, why wouldn't you be?), then you will have come across this argument. It's one that I think has particular force because it works so well against the large number of religious anti-choice advocates, many of whom seek to change laws to inhibit women's rights to bodily autonomy, and many do the dirty groundwork of standing at picket lines and harassing people who make the difficult decision to get an abortion.

I use the term "anti-choice" now to refer to people whom I used to call "pro-life". I don't call them the latter anymore because they are not pro-life but pro-birth – they don't care about the baby after it is born. They don't care about its life chances as a growing human and working for the success in life of all those babies they demand being born. Indeed, such activists are often against social welfare systems and networks of support. To be "pro" something sounds very positive and I don't think these people are particularly positive in anything about their behaviour.

I do not want to derail this argument by having a very in-depth discussion about what *life* or *personhood* is. So I will be throwing myself into the thick of the argument. If you want to look more at the foundational philosophy that might well underwrite ideas about when life or personhood starts, I have written extensively on this elsewhere, so knock yourself out.[1]

---

[1] See my piece "What Is Personhood? Setting the Scene.", for example, at *A Tippling Philosopher*, https://www.patheos.com/blogs/tippling/2017/11/11/person hood-setting-scene/ (accessed 21/10/2021), as one example.

It sounds controversial and counter-intuitive, but…God loves abortion!

Or, it is necessary for foetuses to die for a greater good. You can already see how this continues in the same vein as the last argument.

Well, that's certainly one of the conclusions that must come from the statistics for natural, spontaneous abortions, or miscarriages. These are abortions that God has the power to stop, and seemingly designed into the system in the first place in actualising this biological world.

Technically speaking, a *spontaneous abortion* is the "noninduced embryonic or foetal death or passage of products of conception before 20 weeks gestation".[1] If this happens after twenty weeks, this is often known as a *stillbirth* or *foetal demise.*

And it happens a lot. Both types.

The statistics for miscarriages are notoriously difficult to assess accurately. This is mainly due to the fact that many spontaneous miscarriages go unreported since they often simply go unnoticed by the mother.

So why am I writing about this? Because, statistically, it means that anywhere up to 75% of all pregnancies, of all fertilised eggs, die. This is a staggering number of pregnancy losses (for example, it is estimated that three out of four eggs that are fertilised do not fuse their DNA correctly, and therefore either do not attempt to implant or fail at implantation). Of course, being exact on these numbers is rather academic, and arguably impossible. Most estimates are almost certainly on the conservative side. Nevertheless, whether it be fifty million a year in the US or twenty million or even a completely unrealistic one million is irrelevant since all these numbers are ridiculously high when anti-choice advocates argue that each one is a *human being*![2]

The reason for talking about this is twofold. First, for people who critique abortion on religious grounds, it makes somewhat of a mockery of their arguments.

---

[1]   "Spontaneous Abortion", *MSD Manual Professional Version*, https://www.msdmanuals.com/en-gb/professional/gynecology-and-obstetrics/abnormalities-of-pregnancy/spontaneous-abortion (accessed 21/10/2021).
[2] They are not, of course.

Second, again from a religious perspective, it does make God look a little callous. Nay, brutal and unloving.

Let's explore these issues.

God is supposedly omnipotent (all-powerful) and omnibenevolent (all-loving). In that context, let's look at the standards that Christians adopt when approaching abortion, and then when they evaluate their perfect God. The religious anti-choicer will take the general approach that abortion is the murder of human beings. If this is the case, then the death, at the hands of other humans, of any and every embryo from blastocyst onwards, is bad, abhorrent, murder, and so on.

Given this appraisal of the ethics of abortions, let us then look at the God scenario, from whence Christians obtain their morality.

Let us assume that somewhere between 60% and 75% of human embryos are fertilised and subsequently die naturally. As mentioned, the numbers aren't so relevant, though the sheer volume does make you stop and think a little harder. This raises these points:

(1) OmniGod has the ability to stop this from happening.

(2) By allowing it *passively*, God is actually *implicitly* declaring that the deaths serve a greater good.

(3) The manner in which these deaths serve a greater good is necessary for this greater good. In other words, there can be no other way with less suffering that this greater good can come about; otherwise God, as an all-loving being, would have chosen the alternative option.

(4) The vast majority of these deaths go unknown to most everyone in the world. Thus the deaths can have nothing to do with humanity and our "journey" – teaching or paying us back for something This prompts the question as to exactly how they can serve such a "greater good" purpose.

(5) Since these deaths occur on such a scale, and no decent reason is forthcoming, then perhaps foetal life isn't as sacrosanct as many like to claim.

The standard Christian response to issues such as these (which fall into the category of the Problem of Evil – why is there so much suffering on Earth given OmniGod's characteristics?) is to offer the "Omniscience Escape Clause", as minister turned atheist author John Loftus has often talked about:[1]

> We've heard this escape clause so many times before. "My ways are not your ways," an ancient superstitious canonized Biblical text says of God. "How do we know what an omniscient God might do?" an apologist chimes in. It could be how God purportedly communicated to us in ways that are indistinguishable from anything else we see in the ancient world, or the tragedy of the Haitian earthquake, or a child suffering and soon to die from Leukemia. How can we judge an omniscient God's ways we're asked over and over, with an implied "We can't." The answer is obvious. We must be able to understand enough of God's ways to know that his ways are good and that he knows what he's doing. It's that simple. If God does not act as a loving person would do then all we can reasonably conclude is that God is not acting like a loving person would do. And if God does not respond in discernible loving ways when tragic events take place then it looks entirely as if tragic events happen randomly without his ever-watchful eye.

This is also known as *skeptical theism* and posits that we cannot know the mind of God, or we would not understand the reasons as to why such evil must exist. This again raises the question as to what kind of reason could be beyond our comprehension, and what kind of reason could actually justify death on such a massive scale. Even if, by some appeal to our idiocy, we cannot understand because of cognitive deficiency why these deaths must occur, then it would be appropriate

[1] Loftus, John W. (2010), "The Omniscience Escape Clause", *Debunking Christianity*, http://debunkingchristianity.blogspot.co.uk/2010/07/omniscience-escape-clause.html (accessed 21/10/2021).

for God to at least let us know *that these deaths aren't in vain*, that they *do* provide a mechanism for achieving a greater good. Some kind of revelation, one way or another, would be decent. "Okay humans, I know that you won't understand why I have designed the world so that these foetal 'human beings' die, but let me at least be clear with you: there *is* a reason."

What we come to, as a conclusion to this scenario, is one or some of these propositions:

(a) either God is not omnibenevolent
(b) or God does not exist
(c) and/or embryos are not so sacred and arguments over what defines personhood are called for
(d) or that millions of foetal deaths a year, unknown to humanity, are necessary for a greater good, but we need to be kept in the dark about what that greater good looks like.

Of all those options, the last one is by far the most improbable, and yet it must be the one adhered to by most, if not all, Christians (whether they recognise this or not).

I challenge Christians to defend this allowance in light of pro-life ethics. And please don't resort to the "we can't know the mind of God" feebleness as wrapped up in the Omniscience Escape Clause.

5 – God Is Morally Culpable for Our Sins (and Atonement Is Incoherent)

The previous arguments have laid the groundwork for this one. We continue with the idea that God is not a good designer, and that any fault with its design is the responsibility of the designer. After all, that is how we understand design in earthly reality.

As a Christian sidebar, this also makes a mockery of Jesus' supposed atonement for our sins – his sacrifice and death as payment for the sins of humanity. If God, with full divine foreknowledge, designed us, and knew before creation what each and every outcome for each and every human (and non-human) would be (with all the range of sin and mayhem you can possibly imagine), and *then* created us anyway, then God is morally culpable for our sins.

Let me analogise.

Imagine you are an extraordinarily good scientist in your lab. You have concocted a design for a new sentient creature. You know that this creature, if you were to create it, would, *with one hundred percent certainty*, go out and rape and pillage in the local town. These sentient beings (they will be profligate), you *know* they would run amok, freely causing pain and suffering. They would also paint some lovely pictures, and be nice to people at times, too. Knowing all of this, you create them anyway. And the creatures go out from your lab into the wider community and cause the expected mayhem (admittedly, with some moments of loveliness). The police come knocking on your door. They find you ultimately morally culpable for the crimes committed by that which you knowingly designed and created. You are deemed, rightly, to

33

be a meddling, ne'er-do-well scientist with moral responsibility for what you caused to come about, and knew would come about before you took the steps to create.

To continue with analogising, if I were a CEO (and chief designer) at a car company, and I designed a car that I knew would be faulty and would cause death when it malfunctioned, and decided to create that car anyway, releasing it to market, I would be morally and legally culpable for so doing.

If that car were bought by someone and it crashed, causing pain and suffering, and I *knew* it would crash – *why* and *how* it would crash – and I built it in such a way *that* it would crash, then I would and should rightly be held accountable.

These analogies show that God should not be let off the hook for the moral misdemeanours of these imperfect beings called humans. There is no way around this if God has that perfect foreknowledge, that omniscience, and was the ultimate creator of all there is and ever will be. It has chosen to create imperfect beings that it has designed, and whom it knows will cause untold havoc. And yet it is apparently perfect, and morally off the hook?

Or, an ultimate OmniCreator is ultimately responsible.

For *everything*.

6 – Demanding Payment for Its Own Faulty Design

This is where I will be guilty of getting rather Christo-centric. You can take the general idea of this argument to be a necessary extension of the last one. God shouldn't render third parties accountable for that which it has faultily designed and created with the full foreknowledge of what the creations would do. Furthermore, to demand third-party payment (i.e. the death of Jesus or exacting some other such thing) for its own design shortcomings is morally incoherent.

As discussed, God is morally culpable for our hardwired shortcomings. Some theologians and denominations of Christianity (especially) see this as humanity being "depraved". This may have originated from The Fall and the blight of Original Sin (thanks Eve!)[1] or from some other feature of humanity (evolved or designed).

We are all broken, according to Christian doctrine. Without being able to create ourselves (though transhumanism and the future may open up doors here), we are thrust into this world as blastocysts, foetuses, and then babies, only to be labelled broken and sinful.

What a lovely positive vibe that gives off.

In Christianity, there is the bizarre situation of the Atonement. This is where, somehow, Jesus' death is a payment for the sins of humanity. Those sins that emanate from our broken natures.

Let's rewind a little. We have seen that God is ultimately responsible for this situation. God designs and creates all of us knowing exactly what we will do and why (unless all of our behaviour is

---

[1] Yes, that can be interpreted as the casual sexism of the Hebrew Bible.

completely random, it must have some reasonable causality underwriting it). Given this decision to create us despite knowing exactly what will come to pass, God still apparently wants *some kind of payment*.

This is very odd.

Remember the CEO/designer/manufacturer of the car company. Imagine selling a faulty car to someone that you know, by designing it thus, will crash and kill other people after you have sold it. You sell it anyway, and then a few years later, you *demand recompense* for the fact that *your design and creation*, your car, crashed and killed someone due to its faults that you knowingly designed and manufactured. As the CEO *you* feel aggrieved enough to warrant the books being balanced back in your favour.

That's how incoherent the Atonement is. So it's no wonder that, after two thousand years, theologians still can't agree on how it works. There is a good dozen theories of Atonement, and they are pretty much mutually exclusive!

The same theorising can be applied to punishing people in hell. But we will circle back to this later.

7 – Why Don't We Photosynthesise?

It turns out that mere existence is predicated upon a whole raft of pain and suffering. Many organisms require the pain and death of other organisms in order to *simply exist*. This happens, literally, on an industrial scale, from the Serengeti to modern intensive farming. I once watched an online video of a water buffalo being eaten alive by a pride of lions just so I could understand this point in its full horror. (Actually, truly understanding it would be to experience being torn limb from limb whilst still being alive.)

It was terrible.

But that's life – or death, as may be. And it has happened for a very long time. All that pain and suffering – every unit – has been built into the design of so many organisms. Nature is red in tooth and claw. Just how God intended it to be.

Humans feel pain. Luckily, we've become clever enough and good enough at using tools to not be part of the food chain (usually). Other animals aren't so lucky. And, despite what some apologists might try to tell you, they *do* feel pain. And they die.

But it does not have to be that way. OmniGod could have made it any other way, surely, with its omni-skills? Carnivorousness can't be necessary, can it? We could, for example, all photosynthesise. All organisms could derive all of their energy from the sun, thus not necessitating the death of other animals.

We already know of certain organisms that can do this – the Oriental hornet can harvest solar energy, and so can plants (of course) – so it's not a stretch to suggest that God could have designed animals to be able to photosynthesise.

God could either create the physical constant to allow for this so that we could generate enough energy from the sun to do what we do. Or simply allow for perpetual miracles to take place in every organism.

OmniGod could do perpetual miracles. This is a really nifty tool for getting God out of these problematic corners. Yet, what it really looks like is a physical and naturalistic world that has all of its problems and foibles, oddities and shortcomings. But the theist has to explain each and every one of them in light of OmniGod – the universe is jam-packed full of these problematic corners that theists have to argue themselves out of. Why do we need this much energy, and why can't we get it from the sun? Why do we and other animals have to get it from the death of still other animals?[1] And, while you're at it, black holes. What's going on there?

You can take this a step further. Maybe we don't actually need energy. God could have created organisms, or a whole system, that didn't revolve around our understanding of energy. This may sound bizarre to the naturalist, but we can throw out all of our frameworks and how we think universes have to work, because God is OmniGod! We (all living entities) wouldn't have to be scrabbling, fighting, competing amongst and with each other to merely survive if we didn't require energy. God could have created otherwise, or could simply play the perpetual miracle card.

Further, God did not need to create a physical world at all. God could just have created heaven, and populated heaven directly. There's a thought. A thought to which we will later return.

---

[1] This is where I smugly announce that I'm vegan.

8 – God Has No Free Will

I don't believe in free will. Well, *libertarian free will* as so defined: The real, rational and conscious ability to do otherwise in any given scenario, all things remaining equal.

I have written an awful lot on this – a book, two book chapters, and countless blog articles. I'm in good company since the vast majority of philosophers deny the existence of libertarian free will (simply "free will" from henceforth), and it turns out that the only ones who embrace this version of free will are pretty much those who believe in God as well.

But more on that in a later chapter on free will concerning humans.

It might seem strange that I include a chapter on free will in the context of God before the main chapter about free will, but for the purposes of this argument, let us assume that this version of free will exists.

Many theists will say that God must have free will because it appears to be a "great-making property" (in this case, in terms of human characteristics). The idea is that humans are endowed with it, and it indeed explains at least a lot of suffering. The suffering of murder and rape and genocide comes about through the bad decisions made by humans exercising their free will. This evil is explained and justified – and essentially trumped – by us humans exercising free will. It is *that* good of a characteristic that it outweighs all of the bad it can bring about. Being such a powerful tool – a great-making property – surely God must have it.

And this makes intuitive sense because one imagines, from a believer's point of view, that God *freely decides* to do things, but really could *not* do them if it so desired.

The problem, and this is a genuine issue for free will as a concept as it applies to humans as well, is that what God desires is itself determined by its nature.

With humans, there is a distinctive difference: We are not bound by abstract requirements of having to be all-loving. And we certainly don't know everything, least of all every future event that will come to pass. In fact, *all* of God's omni-characteristics constrain its *actions*.

I use the word *action* here because I don't think God can make *decisions*. I don't think God can choose to do otherwise in a rational and conscious manner in any given situation. Making decisions entails deliberation – thinking about outcomes and weighing the consequences. God doesn't need to spend time thinking and deliberating, weighing up and evaluating.

God is perfect. God is all-loving. God knows everything. God has no need to waste time deliberating or calculating. God *knows* what the most loving thing to do would be and *must* do what is most loving. With an array of different options potentially available to it, God is unable to choose to do that which is not the most loving, it is a case of automatically doing that which is the most loving in order to fulfil its characteristics and its own once-future predictions about itself and what it would do.

To make sense of freely choosing one option over another, an agent must be uncertain over the various options. The agent deliberates over which one to go for, thus giving the decision some rationale. But if you *know* what you are going to ~~decide~~ do indubitably in advance of doing it, you cannot "make a decision". You are merely *acting*. Therefore, free will and omniscience are incompatible.

God is rather like a divine robot, destined to do only that which its programming allows, with the programming being the fulfilment of omni-characteristics. Anything that falls outside of that remit is invalidated.

I have had theists reply to me, when I point out that God countenanced rape in the Hebrew Bible, that God *wouldn't* do that – *couldn't* do that – because of its nature.

Well, yeah. That's the point – OmniGod's nature is not based on free will, and its free will is constrained like train tracks constrain a train trolley by its nature. All I am doing here is taking that idea and running with it. To the finishing line.

Finally, God's free will is also further curtailed since with its omniscience, it cannot act contrary to its own predictions. For example, if you were omniscient and omnipotent and you predicted that you would make yourself spaghetti Bolognese for supper on Friday, then when it came to making Friday's supper, you would have no choice but to make spaghetti Bolognese. This is because if you decided to be contrary to your own prediction and cook, say, pizza, then your (supposedly infallible) prediction would have been incorrect. This would render your omniscience faulty, and would leave you with the characteristic of fallibility.

Likewise, God does not have omnipotence, because it cannot do something that would invalidate its infallible predictions. Or, looking from another point of view, God is entirely constrained by its own foreknowledge, which, as mentioned, would surely apply to God itself. Thus, God has no *real* and *actual* ability to do otherwise.

So, logically, God can never be contrary to its own predictions. This has far-reaching consequences: God does not have free will, intercessory prayer is pointless, God cannot change its mind, God's own future and interferences on Earth are determined, and the passage in the Bible where Yahweh changed his mind over the fate of Nineveh is patently false (Jonah 3:10).

After all, in God's nature "there is no change or shadow of alteration" (James 1:17).

If you are feeling a bit biblically inclined, here are a few more that show God's lack of free will and thus lack of omnipotence:

> ...the fact that His purpose is unchangeable... (Hebrews 6:17)

It is impossible for God to lie. (Hebrews 6:18)

...in the hope of eternal life, which God, who cannot lie, promised long ages ago... (Titus 1:2)

"God cannot be tempted by evil, and He Himself does not tempt anyone." (James 1:13)

"If we are faithless, He remains faithful, for He cannot deny Himself." (2 Timothy 2:13)

9 – God and This World Are Immutable

Again, the following ideas here are essentially a continuation of the previous ones, whilst adding some more nuance.

OmniGod is omniscient and infallible. It knows everything and it cannot make mistakes. It also has full divine foreknowledge, according to such theists.

Another claim we hear is that God is also immutable – unchanging. This would be consistent with the other attributes above. And I have no problem with this given all the other characteristics involved.

I have already discussed that God cannot have free will since God is constrained by its own characteristics, and this world must be a perfect world (in some way), being the perfect creation of an omnibenevolent, omniscient god.

With God's infallible foreknowledge, this means that God's predictions or knowledge about how the world will be cannot be wrong. Thus, from the moment of creation of space and time, God would know how the world would turn out to be – from the first nanosecond to the last.

The ramifications of God's foreknowledge are interesting. First, it arguably shows that we individuals do not have free will because it appears that we can only act in one given way. Theistic libertarian free willers claim that God isn't *causing* us to act in a given way, it just knows what we will *freely* do. Hmmm.

There are many problems with this. Let us start with the *grounding objection*: For us to do A in a certain scenario and not ~A, but ~A in a different hypothetical scenario and not A, it must be grounded in some causality or reasoning for God to know this and for it not to be random. There must be *something* about the scenario that causes A. It can't be grounded in God because that would mean *theological determinism* – God causing events to be as they are. But the theist doesn't want the actions to be grounded in the causal circumstance or scenario, because this looks like ordinary causal determinism, and the theist claims we must be free! Likewise, an action cannot be grounded in the last variable here – the individual – for a number of reasons, as the *Internet Encyclopedia of Philosophy* points out:[1]

> However, they also cannot be grounded in the individuals to which they refer for at least four reasons. First, counterfactuals of creaturely freedom are true prior to the existence of the individual to which they refer. Second, the existence of the individuals is dependent upon the will of God, and therefore, the truth of the counterfactuals would also be dependent upon the will of God (which has already been shown to be problematic). Third, counterfactuals, properly speaking, refer to non-actual states of affairs and therefore, the events to which they refer never happen, and fourth, psychological makeup cannot serve as grounding because this suggests that the actions performed are not free and thus, the propositions describing the decisions/actions cannot be deemed counterfactuals of freedom.

In fact, any variables that are deferred to in the individual (such as genetics, biology, and psychology) are off-limits for grounding because they merely invite causal determinism whereby the grounding of the foreknowledge is in knowing all the causal determinants of a decision or action, including those of the make-up of the individual.

So we have a bizarre situation of God knowing all creaturely decisions made in the universe from beginning to end, but the theist

---

[1] Laing, John D., "Middle Knowledge", *Internet Encylcopedia of Philosophy*, https://iep.utm.edu/middlekn/ (accessed 03/11/2021).

claiming the knowledge can't be grounded in the individual or the causal circumstance, and neither directly caused by God. This divine foreknowledge appears to render the idea of our free will incoherent (more on this later). But it also invalidates God's own free will because *it cannot act contrary to its own predictions about its own behaviour.* Given that God can only create in a way that fulfils its own omni-nature, and given that God can do only one thing (what God has infallibly predicted) and humans can do only one thing (what God has infallibly predicted), then this world must just be a set of unerring dominoes falling down in a pattern set out from the outset.

Nothing can change – not God's mind, not God's decisions, not human decisions, nothing about the world or reality – from how God imagined and predicted it back at the very beginning. If you are a theist who believes in such a god, just think about that for a while. Consider the ramifications.

God is immutable – unchanging and unchangeable. And so is human behaviour and the world at large. Perfectly so. God can't be surprised about it, either: the universe is a clockwork machine playing out in the exact manner and to the exact outcomes that it designed and created.

Either that, or God doesn't exist. Or God is not OmniGod.

Jonathan MS Pearce

Part Two

WHY WE BELIEVE (OR NOT)

The reasons *why* we believe are far more pertinent than the content of *what* we believe when we are interested in changing people's minds. As the old maxim goes: you can't reason someone out of a position they never originally reasoned themselves into.

Belief is a psychological thing. We generally *don't* believe things like whether or not God exists *after* neutrally observing all of the facts and arguments concerning the subject and *then* reaching the conclusion to believe one way or the other. Instead, we often believe what our parents believe, or what we intuitively believe, or what we want to believe for psychological reasons. And then we spend the rest of the time *post hoc rationalising* (making arguments for a position *after* arriving at the position) and defending that initial irrational or a-rational belief decision.

Non-belief or atheism or secularism (or whatever label you choose) often comes from finally realising these arguments exist after a gradual process of niggling questions and doubts biting away at the edges. But it can equally come from a life-changing psychological event – a death, a divorce, a job loss. That said, such events can also send a believer into a more consolidated belief than they previously had.

And this can happen in reverse, from non-belief to belief. It's just that, statistically, the traffic is very much one-way. In America, the UK, and other developed nations, non-belief is a growing demographic and it is far more likely that someone will deconvert from religion to atheism or agnosticism *and stay there* than will convert from atheism to religion *and stay there.*[1]

Belief in God or a god or gods is a complex thing that involves all manner of variables from psychology and rationality (philosophy) as mentioned, but also culture, society, community, history, and so on.

Interestingly, the countries in the world with the most existential security – the least violence (war and crime), the most effective welfare systems, the greatest education, the most certainty about their future – have the lowest levels of religiosity.[2]

People in war-torn countries, whose lives are threatened continuously and who live in perpetual uncertainty, have a greater adherence to religion and belief in God(s). Because God, for them, provides some functional benefits.

The fact that there are so many variables affecting each of our belief systems should not take away from the important one for anyone like myself: philosophy – rational argumentation.

Bear with me a short while as I explain another reason people believe – well, more accurately, keep believing. Richard Dawkins, Susan Blackmore, and others have previously expressed the idea that memes are analogous to genes. I think this is a useful analogy as to how memes continue to exist (though there are many detractors, but I don't think my basic idea is particularly controversial). What is a meme? This is how I see it (not necessarily anyone else!), and broken down for easy digestion. A meme is an idea, and ideas exist because they convey some kind of advantage to their users, or have survival mechanisms, such as we might understand with genes in biology. Ideas either adapt to their environment, or they die out because they convey no advantage to the organisms (humans) who hold them (think).

---

[1] Such data is variously available, such as in Merion, Stephen (2012)," Irreligious Socialization? The Adult Religious Preferences of Individuals Raised with No Religion", *Secularism & Nonreligion*, 1, p. 1-16, https://secularismandnonreligion.org/articles/abstract/10.5334/snr.aa/ (accessed 17/11/2021).

[2] For example, see the Global Peace Index, information about which can be found at its entry on *Wikipedia*, https://en.wikipedia.org/wiki/Global_Peace_Index (accessed 22/11/2021).

In more recent years, memes on the internet convey humour or a poignant message, and so people who enjoy them pass them on to others. These ideas continue to exist because they have a competitive advantage over ones that "die out".

In the case at hand, imagine a memeplex – a whole network of ideas – such as a religion. Why might the belief in a religion like Christianity maintain over time? What advantage or survival mechanisms might it give or have?

For starters, religions provide social function for adherents – a sense of identity that binds a tribe together and builds social cohesion. There is also attribution. Religious adherents can attribute divine explanation to things humans do not yet understand in terms of natural causes. Alternatively, even if humans *do* understand the workings of nature, those religionists can refuse to accept the outcome by attributing it to the will or existence of God. There might also be the idea, again wrapped up with social cohesion, that the religion also underwrites moral codes that bind the community together.

So on and so forth.

But the other very powerful characteristics that many of these popular religions so ubiquitously have are something I call *memetic failsafes*. These failsafes are heaven and hell.

Heaven is the single most amazing thing in human conception. When you ask someone what heaven is (because it is not actually prescriptively laid out by most holy books), it ends up being the greatest place, the greatest end result, that they can possibly imagine.

The same reasoning applies to hell. It is literally the worst thing, place, end result that a human being can possibly conceive.

Or, heaven is the greatest carrot, and hell the greatest stick, humanly imaginable.

What this means is that religions that use these twin ideas have them as memetic failsafes that lock people into the religion beyond rational boundaries. It might be that you have a problem with certain aspects of Christianity, but to let these deconvert you is to deny yourself access to heaven (the greatest place in human conception to which you will surely be going) and possibly condemn you to hell (the worst place in human conception).

Oh dear. You might as well keep believing.

Add to these other (softer) failsafes, like social networks that keep the believer locked in, and it becomes really difficult to leave a religion. In Bible Belt America, if you leave your church and deconvert, you are often ostracised by your community – family and friends – and left out in the cold. You may even lose your job.

In Afghanistan, you may lose your head.

In this way, the threats are not only conceptual – promissory notes of a heaven or hell – but real. Very, very real.

It's a version of Pascal's Wager, but one that really does operate ubiquitously at the back of believers' minds as well as in their daily lives.

What is Pascal's Wager? Well, it is the famous argument for why you should believe, on balance and surveying the four options available to you, as I interpret it here:

	Belief that God exists	**Belief that God does not exist**
God actually exists	**Epic win (heaven)!** Infinite gain.	**Epic loss (hell)!** Infinite loss.
God does not actually exist	Meh.	Meh.

We could add to this Carroll diagram the realities for some people in their communities, as mentioned above:

	Belief that God exists	**Belief that God does not exist**
God actually exists	**Epic win of heaven!** Infinite gain.	**Epic loss of hell!** Infinite loss. **Potential earthly death, loss of social network, job, family, friends.** Earthly loss.
God does not actually exist	**Potential earthly gain of not being killed, maintaining social network, etc.** Earthly gain.[1]	**Potential earthly death, loss of social network, job, family, friends.** Earthly loss.

What you can see is that heaven and hell help to lock people into the belief that God exists. And this is further exacerbated by very tangible, real-world consequences.

There are some serious problems with Pascal's Wager, not least that "belief in God" is not your only god option. There may be as many as 4,200 religions in the world, and 42,000 different denominations of Christianity alone! So getting it right is not simply believing in God or not – you need to get the *right* god!

I digress.

The point is, people believe often for psychological reasons and are then locked into those beliefs by conceptual bribery.

Atheism is a tough sell. You die, and you're worm food, or ashes. Or if you are being even more useful, being picked apart by a medical student or researcher. And probably then worm food or ashes.

Whoop! That gets them flocking to the atheist church.

---

[1] This is mainly relevant in countries where nonreligion is not normative, and atheists are in an oppressed minority.

The thing is, reality is reality. It's not a dressed-up marketing manager's dream project; it just is. So I understand why there are still so many believers in the world at a time of such plentiful scientific discovery, understanding, and enlightenment.

If humans were to be rational, however – strictly rational – I think religion would end up being adhered to by the tiny minority in society. If religion didn't have these psychological draws – these memetic failsafes – and we were evaluating the claims on a purely rational basis, religion would struggle to maintain a foothold in society.

In this next series of arguments, we look in finer detail at some of the issues pertaining to belief, and the activity of persuading people into a religion. Or, as we will see, being born into it.

10 – The Accidents of Geography and History

Counter-apologist and philosopher of religion, John W. Loftus, wrote an excellent book called *The Outsider Test for Faith*. The argument in this chapter will borrow from that book to some degree. It is a great book, like all of his other works, and one I suggest you read.

As I have already hinted, there are many variables that are involved in why people believe in God, most of which are not particularly rational. The accidents of geography and history are prominent ones.

The simple fact of the matter is that there is tremendous religious diversity in the world. But that diversity is ghettoised – isolated or segregated by place or group. The distribution of religion is not random. This is how John Loftus sees it (p. 33):[1]

> [P]eople who are located in distinct geographical areas around the globe overwhelmingly adopt and justify a wide diversity of mutually exclusive religious faiths due to their particular upbringing and shared cultural heritage. This is the Religious Diversity Thesis (RDVT), and it is a well-established fact in today's world. The problem of religious diversity cries out for a reasonable explanation, something that faith has not provided so far.

---

[1] Loftus, John W. (2013), *The Outsider Test for Faith: How to Know Which Religion Is True*, Amherst, NY: Prometheus Books.

The size of these groups is also diverse. We have 2.1 billion Christians and 1.5 billion Muslims, compared to 23 million Sikhs and 4 million Shintoists. And everyone in between and in even smaller religions. We have a further problem in that a given religion will itself be split into different denominations. For instance, Christianity has some 42,000 different denominations largely based on geographical and historical distribution, and often having a variety of competing or conflicting beliefs.

Why is this a problem? As an example, if you were an Arab born in Riyadh, Saudi Arabia in 1996, you are incredibly unlikely to be a Hindu; indeed, it is almost certain that you will grow up being a Muslim. Likewise, you are unlikely to have primal-indigenous beliefs of the power of the Amazon River growing up in a Lutheran community in Bible Belt USA. Parents, families, communities and societies so often define who we become and what we believe.

There are, and this is an indisputable fact, distinct geographical concentrations of religions around the world. Christians may be concentrated in Europe, South and North America, and other pockets of colonial history. Islam prevails in the Middle East, North Africa, parts of subcontinental India, and the islands of the Indian Ocean. Shintoists primarily exist in Japan, and Hindus in India. These and other statistical generalisations and trends exist.

If God were perfectly loving, then it would ensure that all people could participate in a relationship with God unless people had somehow deliberately excluded themselves through some kind of resistance. Some philosophers call the people who under other circumstances would have happily believed in the right god given the right context *nonresistant nonbelievers*. They don't believe in the right god not because they are wholly against the idea of that god, necessarily, but because they just weren't lucky enough to be in the right geographical and/or historical context.

The challenge for religionists is that most religions have it wrong. That is, religions are mutually exclusive. If I am a Muslim, I believe that the Muslim religion and revelation are correct, and I believe my religion is a more accurate representation of reality than that which a Jainist believes (almost certainly) in India. And if access to heaven or hell, or nirvana, or whatever afterlife there is, or if access to God (whichever god exists), or if access to the fruits of belief in the correct god, depends upon *believing* in the correct god, then there is a lot on the line.

However, given the serious implications of belief, it seems rather bizarre that OmniGod would design, create and arrange the world (or allow the world to develop) in such a way that *most people* don't rationally survey the smorgasbord of religious offerings and then, using logic and reason, assent to the correct one. Instead, they are *overwhelmingly born into* any given religion.

The belonging to a particular religion depends on where and when they were born. And that might well be the component of their existence that informs the verdict of whether or not they access the good stuff or get condemned to the bad stuff. Perhaps for eternity. (It must be remembered that I am generalising here for simplicity, and that the range of religions have a range of beliefs concerning afterlife and divine reward and punishment.)

As Loftus continues (p. 37-38):[1]

> The main problem religious diversity presents us with is that not every religious faith can be true. In fact, given the number of mutually exclusive religious faiths in the world, it's highly likely that the one you inherited in your respective culture is false (given the odds alone)....
>
> Robin McKim tells us that it "is clear, therefore, that large numbers of people have held, and now hold false beliefs in the area of religion...at most one of them can be true....And since so many people hold false beliefs in the area of religion, it would seem, therefore, that all groups need to consider the possibility that their beliefs in this area may be mistaken."

---

[1] Ibid.

It gets worse when you consider the vagaries of history. Imagine being born into Egyptian or Aboriginal Australian culture in 5,000 BCE, before the events of the Hebrew Bible or the Christian Bible (i.e., Old and New Testaments). Now imagine that Christianity is the one true religion. How is it fair, when one has no control over when and where one is born, that one is born into one of those contexts? The person would have absolutely no chance of being able to access the correct divine revelation upon which rests the reward of heaven or the punishment of hell.

This presents arguably three options for the theist:

(1) Even though people end up believing the wrong religion, largely outside of their control, they can still access the good stuff (heaven, or somehow some kind of union with the correct god…).

(2) God rearranges the world such that the soul of a person who is not able to access the correct god is already known by God to be a soul that would "freely" reject it. So God front-loads that soul into someone who would have no access to this correct god anyway. Throwing out the trash before the movie begins, so to speak.

(3) God really did give secret individual revelations to those people born in the wrong times and places, so it's all okay really.

These options are, evidently, a trifle problematic. For option (1), the corollary of this defence is that we don't really need to believe in the right religion in order to get to heaven (or similar). In the context of Christianity, this might mean that I don't need to have faith in Jesus in order to get to heaven. I can be an Aboriginal Australian or a Muslim or an atheist and still get into Christian heaven presumably because I am a good human being. In other words, it's about the deeds – the works – and not faith in Jesus and the (other aspects of the) Christian God.

I think an awful lot of Christians would have a problem with this.

Most religions seem to operate on a platform of "believe our religious doctrine, the correct one, or you're in trouble" rather than "it doesn't really matter what you believe, as long as you are a good person". Of course, for people like myself, the latter option is far more appealing. It's about having a world full of good people.

The second option above, as espoused by (for example) Christian apologists like William Lane Craig,[1] is, I think, fairly egregious. We will actually return to it fairly soon when considering heaven and hell. But in the meantime, it looks something like this, as set out by theist Tim Stratton:[2]

> God knew that those who never hear the Gospel would freely choose to reject it, even if they did hear it! Remember that God has perfect omniscience; therefore, He knows with certainty who would freely accept His offer of love, and who would freely choose to reject Him even if they could do otherwise. Since God knows who would freely choose to reject Him (even though they really could do otherwise), why does God even need to let them hear the Gospel, since He knows they would reject it anyway?
>
> I can imagine this unevangelized person face to face with Jesus on Judgment Day. This person might initially object and say, "But this isn't fair! How could I have rejected you, when I didn't even know about you?" God would reply, "I knew that even if you were face to face with me on earth, that you would have rejected me anyway." The defendant would then reply, "That's right, I would have rejected you then, and I reject you now!"
>
> God can make sure that those who would repent if they hear the gospel message will hear the gospel message. As an

[1] "What About Those Who Have Never Heard?", *Reasonable Faith with William Lane Craig*, https://www.reasonablefaith.org/media/reasonable-faith-podcast/what-about-those-who-have-never-heard (accessed 21/10/2021).
[2] "What About Those Who Have Never Heard About Jesus?" *Free Thinking Ministries*, https://freethinkingministries.com/what-about-those-who-have-never-heard-about-jesus/ (accessed 21/10/2021).

> advocate of God's middle-knowledge, I believe that God
> knows with perfect certainty who would repent after hearing
> about Jesus. Therefore, if hearing the Gospel is necessary to
> be saved, God can make sure that those He knows would
> accept Him will be born in a time and a place in which they
> will hear the Gospel.

If God, with ultimate control and knowledge, knew that an entity it created would indubitably reject it, then in creating that entity *God is creating a human so that they go to hell* (or similar).

I don't think either of these three options gets the theist out of a bind. They are not good enough and look rather like desperate ad hoc rationalisations.

I would offer a fourth option to the ones listed above: universalism. This is the idea that everyone is eventually saved, one way or another. If I were to be religious, this would definitely be the option I would take. I can make no sense of God at all, but if there were a god, this god and religion would be universalist. If I were God, *everyone* would eventually get the good stuff. After all, it would be my fault for knowingly designing and creating them in the wrong contexts anyway.

But with most versions of God as we understand them, and given religious exclusivity, the scenario presented in this argument is as follows:

(1) Our beliefs will define whether we get the good stuff or don't (heaven, hell, loving union with God, etc.).
(2) Our beliefs (globally) are overwhelmingly defined by when and where we are born.
(3) From (1) and (2), whether we get the good stuff or not is overwhelmingly defined by when and where we are to be born.
(4) We have no control over when and where we are to be born.
(5) Most people are born into the "wrong" places, where beliefs prevail that preclude them from getting the good stuff.

(6) From (3) – (5), most people, overwhelmingly, have no control over whether they get the good stuff (reward) or not (punishment).

(7) A creator who knowingly designs and creates a world in which human beings are punished for something they have no control over is an unjust creator.

(8) God, being ultimately powerful and responsible, has control over everything – when and where we are to be born, the entire world into which we are to be born, who is to be rewarded and punished, and how, etc.

(9) God designs and creates a world in which it knowingly allows most people to overwhelmingly have no control over the good stuff or not.

(10) God knowingly designs and creates a world in which most people are punished and, overwhelmingly, have no control over their punishment.

(11) From (7) – (10), therefore, God is unjust.

One example out of many as to how OmniGod cannot be fair or just, and by not being fair or just, is not omnibenevolent. Thus, if God exists, God is not OmniGod.

11 – Unfair Levels of Evidence

We often hear that God wouldn't put a cross on the moon as overwhelming evidence for his existence because it is just too overwhelming and doesn't give people the "choice" to believe. But this is thoroughly problematic.

This is another argument to show that God is not fair. And, as you have just seen, by not being fair, God does not exist as OmniGod.

We don't need to imagine scenarios like putting a cross on the moon for proof of the existence of God; instead, we can refer back to the Bible itself. Or, to any holy book that gives preferential access to God for one or other protagonist (Moses, Muhammad, Muhammad's entourage, etc.). For this argument, I am going to refer back to Doubting Thomas, one of Jesus' very own Apostles and disciples.

God saw fit to convince Doubting Thomas, who – after all – knew Jesus and saw him do his miracles. He was a disciple – not just any disciple, but one of Jesus' inner circle. And yet *even he* didn't initially believe in the Resurrection, attested to by his friends and eyewitnesses, until he had Jesus standing in front of him and until Jesus made him touch the wounds.

As John 20 relays:

> [24] But Thomas, one of the twelve, who was called Didymus, was not with them when Jesus came. [25] So the other disciples were saying to him, "We have seen the Lord!" But he said to them, "Unless I see in His hands the imprint of the nails, and put my finger into the place of the nails, and put my hand into His side, I will not believe."

26 Eight days later His disciples were again inside, and Thomas was with them. Jesus came, the doors having been shut, and stood in their midst and said, "Peace be to you." 27 Then He said to Thomas, "Place your finger here, and see My hands; and take your hand and put it into My side; and do not continue in disbelief, but be a believer." 28 Thomas answered and said to Him, "My Lord and my God!" 29 Jesus said to him, "Because you have seen Me, have you now believed? Blessed are they who did not see, and yet believed."

And yet almost the entirety of the rest of humanity is not remotely afforded this level of evidence and is expected to believe, arguably on pain of hell.

Thomas got to poke Jesus, bodily resurrected in front of him, in the hands. He got to feel the skin of the real and resurrected God, and only then did he believe.[1]

He's now a Saint.

This is completely unfair and involves terrible double standards.

God is not fair.

Therefore, God is not perfect or omnibenevolent.

The only way God could deal with this potential unfairness is by having some kind of metric for *judgement* that allows for everyone's causal circumstance to be taken into account. Person X believed in God 69% but only with a 32% evidential basis. But what of person Y who believed 90% on evidential basis 12%? And how about person Z who believed on 15% but only had 2% evidential basis? And all combinations thereof.

I'm not sure that this form of metric is either evidenced in the Bible or elsewhere. And I do not know if the classical version of God could use this metric because it would know the outcome in advance

---

[1] Made all the more controversial because Jesus declares that "Blessed are they who did not see, and yet believed" (John 20:29) – these people are to be congratulated for their belief.

anyway and would not need to create the test in order to verify its infallibly predictive knowledge.

I will leave aside the dubious historical accuracy of this pericope. It tells us, though, that the great St Thomas only ended up believing in Jesus' resurrection when presented with first-hand sensory experience of it (evidently the apparent eyewitness testimony of his fellow disciples was not enough).

Yet, for an awful lot of (perhaps almost all) modern potential and actual Christians (and all people throughout time, from Amazonian tribespeople to someone born in Mecca in the 1600s), there is a completely unfair distribution of evidence. Thomas is afforded far more evidence so that he eventually believes (and becomes a saint, no less) than I can *ever* reasonably expect. If the end result of judgement (and heaven or hell) is based on my belief decision without the same experience as Thomas, then this seems even more unfair. And unfortunately, those secluded Amazonians do not even have a Christian option in their "decision".

I or you don't remotely get to cross or even approach that evidentiary threshold or benchmark. All we get is a bunch of people telling us a particular book is the one true book, amongst a whole collection of holy books and revelations from other people and cultures and religions around the world.

And that's it.

I can be no more truly convinced about Christianity by accounts of personal revelation than I can about Islam and Hinduism. Since Christians, Muslims, and Hindus alike (amongst others) purport to receive mutually incompatible revelations, and equally swear by them, an outsider like me cannot take personal revelation claims as reliable reflections of truth. And explicitly philosophical arguments can only really get you to generalised atheism, deism or theism. The Bible is what gets you to *Christianity*.

Yet the Bible is very poor evidence indeed. We have unknown authors, writing in unknown times and unknown places,[1] with

---

[1] Leading us to make educated guesses and inferences.

unknown sources, unverified and unverifiable, writing with evangelising agendas ex post facto,[1] with no historiographical pedigree.

It's shockingly poor evidence.

And I can supposedly go to hell based on whether I choose to believe that very low-level biblical evidence (let's call it 5%). Yet St Thomas (the Apostle) gets to stroll through the pearly gates, one assumes, on the back of *not* believing (assuming the Gospels are true here) even though he is presented with a level of, say, 85%, and Jesus then *reversing* this unbelief (in the Resurrection, Jesus' divinity, and the whole atonement idea – not that Thomas actually would have understood this at the time, I wager) by getting Thomas to poke him, and raising the evidential threshold to 95%!! (Note: I am making these figures up to illustrate my point.)

The Christian believer *could* counter that different people react differently to differing levels of evidence, and concoct some kind of counter-apologetic.

My general point would be, yes, all sorts of people will react differently to the same level of evidence. And all sorts of people get different levels of evidence. It's all a bit of an unfair mess.

Time for another analogy.

Imagine I have a class of 30 children to whom I give a test. All 30 children have different brains, knowledge bases, abilities and thresholds, etc. I give them a test of 100 questions, and declare that the children who fail to get 70/100 will get detention. Children who get 70 will get a special treat.

I then give them a test.

Except, I also give out different cheat sheets to everyone ranging from 0 points of help to 95 points. Each child either gets no extra help or gets some kind of leg up to getting closer to that 70-point success. Some people, like little Thomas, get a cheat sheet with answers worth 95 points. Lucky him.

---

[1] Meaning that they had *already* come to believe that Jesus was the Messiah, *before* coming to write a (not objective) account of his life.

Poor Alice, who is not very clever (due to her genetics and troublesome environment) gets a cheat sheet with 0 points of help, and gets 16/100 and detention.

We could actually make this more ~~sinister~~ accurate: some children are given trickster cheat sheets, like our Saudi student, Mo, who gets a sheet that actually tells him wrong answers, and leaves him with 35 points less than he would have got on his own. He gets 50, and receives a detention.

Perhaps, as a teacher, I actually take in the answers but don't announce to anyone the results until the end of the school day. In the meantime, I plug their results into a matrix that calculates an outcome based on (1) abilities, (2) environment, (3) cheat sheets, and (4) their results. I then use these calculated results to enforce on them a detention or a reward.

That would need some unpicking and looks rather like some kind of deterministic algorithm, the results of which, as this particular teacher (i.e., God), I knew in advance anyway. In other words, creating the test is…pointless. What the algorithm would *actually* produce is everyone getting the same marks since the algorithm would have to be *fair*. There would be no child who would have their environment, genetics, cheat sheet or anything else over which they have no control giving them an advantage or disadvantage.

The only fair option for an OmniGod designing and creating all humanity from nothing is to give everyone the same chance at heaven or hell; and when we control for causal circumstances, this translates to the same score.

Finally, let me bring into play one particular apologist, Catholic Dave Armstrong, who took umbrage with my claims about this, but didn't really hit the mark, as you will see. Here is a snapshot of my blogging world. He said:[1]

---

1 As referenced in Pearce, Jonathan MS (2021), "Doubting the Lessons from Doubting Thomas: Responding to Dave Armstrong Again", *A Tippling Philosopher*, https://www.patheos.com/blogs/tippling/2021/03/18/doubting-the-lessons-from-doubting-thomas-responding-to-dave-armstrong-again/ (accessed 05/11/2021).

> I think God *does* provide sufficient evidence (of all sorts) for every human being, but human beings have various mechanisms by which they rationalize such things away or reject them. If it's not efficient enough to bring about belief (I'm not a Calvinist and believe in human free choices and free will) then one can either criticize God or point out that perhaps the *person* involved has an irrational demand. The fault can conceivably be on either side. God's not to blame for everything (as many of His critics seem to think).

This is actually contradictory. "Sufficient" does not entail a range. Sufficient means "enough for a particular purpose". If I need to put oil in my car for the engine to run, then I put in, say, one litre. *Ceteris paribus*,[1] this is sufficient. Of course, if my car has a hole in a pump somewhere, then this is not sufficient. To get to the next town, I need to put in two litres to overcome the leak. Two litres are the sufficient (i.e., required) amount. One litre *is not sufficient*. It *should* be sufficient if we made inaccurate assumptions about my car by comparing it to another car of the same make and model, but without the leak.

Ceteris paribus.

All other things remaining equal.

But…all other things are not equal. They almost never are.

So, a sufficient amount of oil will change from car to car (as well as the type of oil).

Likewise, sufficient evidence (and type of evidence) for a belief will change from person to person, no matter what the belief you are talking about.

What Armstrong is erroneously saying here is that ten units of evidence that the moon landings never happened is sufficient evidence for Lenny to believe in the conspiracy theory; therefore, ten units of evidence is also sufficient evidence for Julie.

---

[1] A fancy way of saying "all things remaining equal". I used the technical term to give me an excuse to be even more fancy and include another footnote. Win-win.

But Julie is a scientist and a skeptic whose uncle worked on the NASA team. Ten units simply *isn't sufficient* for her.

This is skeptical thinking 101.

Armstrong's contradiction is obvious:

> I think God *does* provide sufficient evidence (of all sorts) for every human being, but human beings have various mechanisms by which they rationalize such things away or reject them.

This should really be translated as:

> I think God does provide sufficient evidence for every human being, but all humans are different meaning that the evidence isn't actually sufficient.

Or A ≠ A.

So it really should be:

> I think God does provide evidence for every human being, but all humans are different meaning that the evidence isn't actually *sufficient*.

Which he almost begrudgingly accepts, and then says of the entity who knowingly created and designed everything in existence in the full knowledge it would do what it would do because it designed it that way:

> The fault can conceivably be on either side. God's not to blame for everything (as many of His critics seem to think).

I utterly contest that claim. God literally designed and created everything in the full knowledge of what could come about. God knew every eventuality, and why it would be, and brought it about anyway. *Of course* God is ultimately to blame.

Doubting Thomas is another example of how easy some have had getting through those pearly gates. And how difficult it is for others. And how unfair OmniGod really is.

12 – Some People Are Still More Likely to Believe than Others, and That's Also Unfair

Fairness is a theme that is running throughout these arguments. It doesn't matter which way you slice and dice it, it is just a fact that certain subgroups of humanity are more likely to believe in God than others. This can be something of a problem.

This is the case with men compared to women, and with certain autistic people compared to neurotypical people. There are other subgroups still. But I will concentrate on these two categories for the sake of brevity.

To start with, I present a fascinating paper – "Mentalizing Deficits Constrain Belief in a Personal God" by Ara Norenzayan, Will M. Gervais and Kali H. Trzesniewski.[1]

The basic conclusion to be made from this work is that people on the autistic spectrum (think particularly Asperger's Syndrome) have, due to their cognitive functioning, a much higher disposition *not* to believe in a personal god. This is largely due, it appears, to a lack of empathy. Empathy, and more particularly *intersubjectivity*,[2] seems to underscore our belief in and beliefs about a personal god. This can be seen in believers needing to put themselves "in God's shoes", so to speak. The ability to put yourself in someone else's shoes is very

---

[1] Norenzayan et al. (2012), "Mentalizing Deficits Constrain Belief in a Personal God", *PLoS One,* 7(5), May 2012, http://www.plosone.org/article/info:doi/10.1371/journal.pone.0036880 (accessed 08/11/2021).
[2] The sharing of subjective experience between two or more people.

important. In other words, in all your words and deeds as a believer, what would God think of you? This intersubjectivity, of placing yourself out of your body and imagining "you" from another point of view, is something that particular groups of autistic people struggle with. And this, it seems, is why they have less propensity to believe.

Of course, they didn't *choose* to be this way.

As the paper states:

> Religious believers intuitively conceptualize deities as intentional agents with mental states who anticipate and respond to human beliefs, desires and concerns. It follows that mentalizing deficits, associated with the autistic spectrum and also commonly found in men more than in women, may undermine this intuitive support and reduce belief in a personal God.

Interestingly, the paper concludes that there are even more variables at play that can affect belief:

> Finally, the prevalence and content of supernatural agent beliefs, although constrained by core social cognitive capacities, respond to and fluctuate with socio-demographic conditions across time and cultures. Within this broader theoretical landscape, these studies present new evidence for a social cognitive mechanism underlying one source of individual differences in religious belief.

There is a similar pattern with men, as opposed to women, being less prone to believing in a personal deity. This fits with other research that shows that women are more empathetic, and that women are more likely to attend church.[1]

---

[1] "Gender profile of church attenders" (2001), *NCLS Research,* https://www.ncls.org.au/default.aspx?sitemapid=137 (accessed 08/11/2021).

Here is an interesting extract from an article discussing this idea, as well as concerning people with autism:[1]

> Men, on average, score worse on the ability to sense emotion (but better on prime numbers, a talent that demands no insight into anyone else's feelings) than do women; and university professors do worse again, while scientists come at the bottom of the list.
>
> People with autism score even lower. Those severely affected live almost detached from the world around them. They lack empathy, concentrate on themselves and may be obsessed with a particular talent (such as being able to tell what day of the week any date will be), combined with loss of other mental abilities. Children with a milder version of the condition, Asperger's syndrome, are often clumsy, shy and tongue-tied.
>
> Others do much better, for they have "high-functioning autism". Such individuals are successful, but have little insight into the emotions of others and often show a deep interest in things mechanical and numerical. The personality type is much more frequent among males than females and, at least in its most severe forms, has a strong genetic component.
>
> On the emotion-sensing tests, those with autism proper do worst, then Asperger's patients, followed by the high-functioning group, and then – in order – by scientists, professors and men. Women come top.
>
> People with autism are mainly interested in the banal reality of what surrounds them and find it hard to consider the abstract world. They are, as a result, highly resistant to the idea of an invisible deity for whom no tangible evidence exists and whose thoughts cannot be penetrated. Teenagers with the condition are far less likely to express a belief in

---

[1] Jones, Steve (2012), "Why Women, Children And Americans Are More Likely To Believe In God", *Insider*, https://www.businessinsider.com/why-women-children-and-americans-are-more-likely-to-believe-in-god-2012-8 (accessed 08/11/2021).

God than their unaffected classmates. The high-functioning group are also much more willing to class themselves as atheists than are their fellows – and, in decreasing order of scepticism, people with autism, Asperger's patients, scientists, professors, men and women (in some studies, men are only half as likely to be believers as are their partners).

Perhaps a logical, systematic and self-centred personality is disposed to doubt, while a more responsive mind is more willing to summon up the divine. Believers are in emotional contact with their deity. They feel that He responds to their prayers, knows their thoughts and guides His subjects in their proper paths. They empathise with their angel and accept what they imagine to be his instructions. Those with autism, scientists and men are happier with their own thoughts.

I want to tread somewhat carefully here as autism is a large umbrella term that encompasses a massive range of people. There will be many exceptions to the claims here, and there are many types of autism that will not fall into the neat categories or conclusions as those shown above. I say this as a father of an autistic child. But the general point holds: certain types of people are less likely to believe in a personal god than other types of people.

As *Live Science* reports, looking at research into higher religiosity amongst women:[1]

A new analysis of survey data finds women pray more often than men, are more likely to believe in God, and are more religious than men in a variety of other ways.

The reasons, analysts say, could range from traditional mothering duties to the tendency of men to take risks – in this case the chance they might not go to heaven.

---

[1] Britt, Robert Roy (2009), "Women More Religious Than Men", *LiveScience*, http://www.livescience.com/7689-women-religious-men.html (accessed 0/11/2021).

The latest findings, released Friday, are no surprise, only confirming what other studies have found for decades. Still, the new numbers illustrate interesting and stark differences. They come from a fresh review of data that was collected in a 2007 survey and initially released last year by the Pew Research Center. The percent of women (and then men) who:

- Are affiliated with a religion: 86 (79).

- Have absolutely certain belief in a God or universal spirit: 77 (65).

- Pray at least daily: 66 (49).

- Have absolutely certain belief in a personal God: 58 (45).

The survey involved interviews with more than 35,000 U.S. adults by the Pew Forum on Religion & Public Life.

As mentioned, it is not important *why* this is the case only *that* it is the case. Some reasons are presented in these sources, but I don't need to consider them for the purposes of this argument. Remember, OmniGod had all the possible worlds it could have created, that it conceptually designed as hypotheticals, and "chose" (or calculated that it was best) to create *this* world.

In this world, rather like the geographical and historical argument seen previously, certain people have more chance of believing in God than other people irrespective of the communities in which they grew up. If God's intention for us, if our objective is to enter into a loving union with God, and if heaven and hell[1] are on the line for us if we do or don't, then it is grossly unfair that the dice are stacked in the favour of some, and against others.

---

[1] If I ever mention these twin bribes of heaven and hell and you think that your religious belief or any other given belief doesn't include some kind of heaven and/or hell, let me emphasise that this refers to any form of reward or benefit, and any kind of punishment, lack of benefit or disadvantage that may be entailed by a belief/lack of belief in God.

God, again, has ultimate design responsibility, and this is yet another design fault (and thus this argument could have fallen in the previous section). It can be formulated into a syllogism:

(1) God is omnibenevolent and will have fairness as a benevolent attribute.

(2) God wants humans to enter into a loving relationship with it.

(3) God has designed people (or the system that designs people) to not have equal fairness and opportunity to access a loving relationship with him.

(4) God also has the power to level the playing field ex post facto but appears not to do so.

(5) God is not fair, and thus not omnibenevolent.

God is not omnibenevolent.

Or, God does not exist.

Part Three

THE MORAL LIFE

Now that God has designed and created life, we are kicking around this here world, trying not to get into trouble.[1] Well, most of us. Some of us get into a lot of trouble, and some of us get away with murder. Literally. A lot. But before we deal with what happens – or supposedly happens – to those who pass the moral test, and those who fail, let's look at taking the test.

Before we investigate morality, we must first look to find a useable definition as to what *morality* is. Let's get philosophical, philosophical![2]

Generally, the study of morality is split into three components: *descriptive morality*, *meta-ethics* and *normative morality*. Often, philosophers replace the term "morality" with "ethics". Descriptive ethics is concerned with what people *actually* believe, morally speaking. Normative ethics (which can be called *prescriptive ethics*) investigates questions of what people *should* believe. Meta-ethics is more philosophical – attempting to define what moral theories and ethical terms actually *refer to*. Or,

- What do different cultures actually think is right? (descriptive)
- How should people act, morally speaking? (normative)

---

[1] But the ones who will, will, and the ones who won't, won't – right, God? Couldn't be any other way…

[2] Yes, this is an Olivia Newton-John reference. Oh dear. My editors begged me to remove this, but I held firm.

- What do *right* and *ought* actually mean? (meta-ethics)

Morality, as the term will be used here, will generally be understood as: "normatively to refer to a code of conduct that, given specified conditions, would be put forward by all rational persons".[1] Translated by me, this is "What people should do according to rational people who've thought a lot about it".

The second important term to attempt to unravel is *objective*. Usually, it means something that is independent of an agent's mind, or mind-independent. This is the understanding I will use here for the sake of argument. Thus, objective morality refers to facts about what constitutes moral behaviour; and these facts lie in the nature of the agent's action, regardless of cultural and individual opinion; and this morality is independent of our minds.

One hugely important question at this point concerns the existence of abstract ideas. I argue that abstract ideas, like morality, *cannot* exist outside of our minds. I think that the idea of abstract ideas outside of our minds is incoherent. I find that theists often end up arguing about ideas like objective morality at only skin depth, at the veneer of philosophy. What theism and theists rely on is some form of (Platonic)[2] realism such that there is a realm where abstract ideas and forms exist. This is not immediately, or even after some critical analysis, apparent.

Indeed, I spent the first part of my book *Why I am Atheist and Not a Theist* setting this out. Go and read that for a greater understanding. I'll try to be quick in summing up here, though.

According to the theist, somehow, out in the aether, (or existing in God, maybe), or however such a *realist* wants to try to establish it, there is the prescriptive form of any given thing in existence. This

---

[1] Gert, Bernard (2011) "The Definition of Morality," *The Stanford Encyclopedia of Philosophy*, 2011. https://plato.stanford.edu/entries/morality-definition/ (accessed July 20, 2013)

[2] Plato argued that perfect forms of things, as abstracts, existed in another "realm" – this we may call platonic realism. Ideas of things in our minds refer to the perfect forms out there, in the aether.

includes morality (but this could also include the *essence of* man, woman, horse, loyalty, hero, table, etc.).

Such (Platonic) thinkers believe that *universals* – universal properties like redness or greenness – exist separately from the particular objects (e.g., apples) that contain said property (greenness, appleness, sweetness, etc.). This is what Platonic realism states. There are other types of realism but let's keep this digestible.

At the opposite end of the spectrum, where I sit, we have the individual conceiving these ideas. As we explore this end of the spectrum, there are two positions that I will explain before conflating them. The first position is *nominalism*.

Nominalism stands in stark contrast to realism in that adherents state that only *particulars* exist, and not universals. Properties of particular objects can account for eventual similarity between objects (such as the green of grass and the green of a painted wall). But universals do not exist. There is no perfect "greenness" as an abstract entity that exists out there and separate from things that are green, but to which the things have some *relation*.

The second position is called *conceptual nominalism* or *conceptualism*. This position states that universals and abstract ideas exist, but only in the *mind of the conceiver*. Thus, if all conceivers were to disappear, the ideas and concepts that they were conceiving would also disappear. If a tree falls in the forest...

If all sentient creatures were to die, then so would the ideas and theories of morality, loyalty, hero-ness, greenness, and so on.

I conceive of green, and see green in many things, and conceptualise the idea of greenness. But my idea of greenness might be different compared to someone else's or to a bat's or cat's or alien's. The same can apply to any abstract: a chair (is that tree stump a chair, is that chair actually a bed for a cat?), a hero (Gandhi, Churchill, Greta Thunberg?), personhood, a right, and so on. When our subjective minds agree on labels, we tend to write dictionaries, encyclopaedias, legal codes, and suchlike.

The point to take away here is that morality is very much an abstract idea, or set of ideas. And it exists in here – in our minds – and not out there, in the aether or in God. When we agree, we write laws, Constitutions, Bills of Rights, Charters of Human Rights, and the like. But people disagree about *them* and even amend *them*. They are conceptually constructed after doing philosophy and arguing.

Let's get back to morality, then.

What are rights, moral laws or morality actually made of? What is their ontology? What are the properties of these abstract ideas? The conceptualist claims, for example, that abstract ideas like morality are concepts in each individual conceiver's mind. Thus, *objective* morality is a non-starter or requires a more befitting definition. (This is not to be confused with the idea that we can underwrite moral claims with objective data about the world.) Because abstract ideas cannot, by definition, be mind-independent, there can be no objective morality.

Now the philosophy gets very in-depth here, but is actually critically important. It is easy to *say* atheists have no ground for objective morality and that theists *do*. But it is a lot harder to *show* how objective morality exists in some kind of mind-independent reality, especially when morality is an abstract concept, and it appears that abstract concepts emerge when minds conceive of things.

Even God can be argued to be an abstraction (since it apparently has *infinite* qualities, a concept that arguably has no *actual* reality). And God is arguably just another mind, so morality looks like it is still subjective. But we will return to these ideas.

This terminology of *objective morality* is ever-present in debates with Christian apologists, as we can see with William Lane Craig's Moral Argument, which he uses in almost every debate:[1]

(1) If God does not exist, objective moral values do not exist.

(2) Objective moral values and duties do exist.

---

[1] E.g., William Lane Craig, "Morality and Does God Exist?", *Reasonable Faith with William Lane Craig,* https://www.reasonablefaith.org/morality-and-does-god-exist (accessed July 20, 2013)

(3) Therefore, God does exist.

There is a philosophical problem here because this might well imply that there must exist some kind of Platonic realm, as mentioned, where these ideas actually exist. It is begging the question: It is circular in smuggling God into the term "objective morality". Without humans in the world, and the actions that carry such moral values, can we actually say that these ideas exist mind-independently?

For example, if one were to posit a moral theory that was universally subjective, such that each rational and knowledgeable person with a sound mind would arrive at the same conclusion in valuing a moral action, would this qualify as "objective"? If ideas and concepts exist only conceptually, rather than *out there* in the *aether*, does the concept of "objectivity" even make sense?

So this is just a fanciful way of smuggling in God.

As atheists, we need to be okay with biting the bullet and saying there is no such thing as objective morality. After all, we can all think of weird and wonderful scenarios where what might seem like an obvious moral decision can be shown to be not so obvious.

This is well summed up with one of the criticisms of Immanuel Kant's Categorical Imperatives. He thought that there are objective moral strictures (this is called *deontology*) that are absolute, such that it is morally wrong to lie, no matter what. But we can think of situations where it might not be so clear. One example is the Inquiring Murderer thought experiment. Imagine Jack and Jill are playing upstairs in your house and the doorbell rings. At the door is a murderer asking where the children, Jack and Jill, are. In this case (all other things remaining equal), it is right (it seems) to lie and claim you don't know where they are in order to save their lives.[1] So there are problems with these objective, absolute, context-independent moral rules.

---

[1] Kant would say that even this scenario would not validate a deliberate falsehood. For him and other such deontologists, lying is *a priori* wrong because it cannot be universally enacted. What would the world look like if everybody lied? This presents, for him, a contradiction in nature.

I have had many conversations with theists who make claims about objective morality without properly defining it and then, upon being pressured, reveal it to mean something like "valid and binding". But this ends up being another circular claim. You cannot have an objective morality without a god since objective morality means a value system validated both instantiated in and bound by some entity. In other words, you can't have "God-derived morality" without God! Well, indeed.

My worldview, in a nutshell, would look something like this:

(1) Abstract ideas only exist in the minds of conceivers, and not in some objective realm.

(2) Therefore, in order to get moral agreement, we need to use moral reasoning and data derived from the world around us, and bring them together to argue for certain moral positions. This is actually evidenced in the world around us because this is actually what we have done and continue to do.

(3) When we agree with each other, we use democratic mechanisms to vote in lawmakers to create laws on our behalf (or have a system of independent lawmakers who operate fairly, with failsafes and checks and balances to ensure this). Again, evidenced in the world around us.

(4) Thus, our moral agreements become laws.

(5) These laws are then enacted and enforced.

(6) The laws can be amended in light of new data or better reasoning.

My worldview is not only how I think morality works, but it is also what really happens (explaining how things can also often go wrong). My moral theories about metaethics and normative ethics cohere with what actually happens in the world – descriptive ethics. What I don't advocate for is reading a 2,000-year-old book from some corner of the world and deriving my moral code and laws from therein because, apparently, "God says so".

The actual reality, for me, is that there is no perfect moral system. I could bore you with the details as to why, but that would require a book-length treatment. Suffice to say that after 3,000 years of moral philosophy, philosophers still don't agree upon which moral framework...works. I am a moral skeptic in that I think we construct our moral philosophies (they don't exist out there in the aether or in God's nature), but none of them are perfect, and they often involve a lot of psychology, too. We make do by arguing, discussing, and hopefully generally agreeing on things.

However, in doing so, we find out that some moral systems are *a lot more wrong* than others. Let's see how this is the case with theistic morality.

13 – Arguments against Divine Command Theory

One of the most common arguments made in defence of theistic morality is *divine command theory*.

As Immanuel Kant would say, we cannot know things in themselves. We don't know what it is to be a bat, or a chair. We can't *know* any thing-in-itself.

That means we use our subjective minds to access *everything*. If God *did* embody moral law in some meaningful way, then we have a whole series of issues. God embodies, in its nature and commands, moral prescriptive law. So we must then interpret what has supposedly been revealed and do what it says in order to be moral ourselves.

The most common version of this is divine command theory (DCT) whereby God's commands determine what is good. In "The Indispensability of Theological Meta-Ethical Foundations for Morality", Christian philosopher and theologian William Lane Craig asserts:[1]

> On the theistic view, objective moral values are rooted in God. God's own holy and perfectly good nature supplies the absolute standard against which all actions and decisions are measured. God's moral nature is what Plato called the

---

[1] Craig, William Lane (1997), "The Indispensability of Theological Meta-Ethical Foundations for Morality", *Reasonable Faith with William Lane Craig*, https://www.reasonablefaith.org/writings/scholarly-writings/the-existence-of-god/the-indispensability-of-theological-meta-ethical-foundations-for-morality/ (retrieved 03/02/2021).

"Good." He is the locus and source of moral value. He is by nature loving, generous, just, faithful, kind, and so forth.

Moreover, God's moral nature is expressed in relation to us in the form of divine commands which constitute our moral duties or obligations. Far from being arbitrary, these commands flow necessarily from His moral nature. In the Judaeo-Christian tradition, the whole moral duty of man can be summed up in the two great commandments: First, you shall love the Lord your God with all your strength and with all your soul and with all your heart and with all your mind, and, second, you shall love your neighbor as yourself. On this foundation we can affirm the objective goodness and rightness of love, generosity, self-sacrifice, and equality, and condemn as objectively evil and wrong selfishness, hatred, abuse, discrimination, and oppression.

God just *has* these qualities. God is a being in a non-spatio-temporal existence (though maybe not after the creation of the universe), and the location of this morality is within God. God somehow grounds these in its nature.

I shall list sixteen arguments against such a position in order to put it to bed. The Christian/DCTer would need to successfully refute all sixteen points for their position to be coherent (these are biblically contextualised). I also use the pronouns "he" and "it" interchangeably when referring to God here. Sometimes it is just easier to visualise the often Christian arguments (pertaining to Yahweh) when using the masculine pronoun:

1. **Arbitrariness** – There is no third-party benchmark and so the idea of goodness becomes arbitrary, even if it is a non-rational assumption made of God. We cannot use some other moral reasoning or scale to morally rationalise God's nature, as this would then become the moral grounding itself, and this process would not necessitate God. But if God is that grounding, what makes its commands good are merely

arbitrary assertions lacking any such rationalisations. Good becomes merely a synonym for God and lacks any useful meaning. Good because God because God is good…

2. **Direction of causality** – The direction of causality works like this: God has lovingness, mercy, kindness etc. But these are not good on their own merit because goodness is rooted in God. These are good *because* God has them. They do not make God good. So if we ask why human lovingness is good, it is because it reflects God, not for any other *reason*. Justice and lovingness are only good on account of God *having* them, not because they obtain any good consequences within or for society, or have intrinsic moral value, or for any other moral reasoning.

3. *We* **are good only because we reflect God** – Think about the previous point on a practical, everyday basis. If you use DCT, then when you are being good, you cannot use moral reasoning to define that goodness, only that it reflects God. Moral reasoning cannot ground morality, because then the grounding would not be in God. This leaves us with a weird scenario such that we cannot provide any reasoning for our own moral actions. "Why is this behaviour good?" cannot be answered in any way other than "because it reflects God's nature". You can't use moral reasoning to teach a child why they are being good other than to appeal, each and every time, to reflecting God. Thus, moral reasoning becomes impotent. It also means that God cannot have reasons for doing as it does, because then it would ground the moral value of the action in moral reasoning outside of God!

4. **Defies everyday moral reasoning and intuition (i.e., consequences)** – An action such as rape is wrong, for us, because of the harm it causes. For the DCTer, it is because

84

God commanded us not to rape. Although, he[1] kind of endorsed it in the Old Testament![2] We say, "Look how horrible rape is! Look at the harm it does." But this in itself does not make it wrong for the DCTer! It carries no intrinsic or extrinsic moral value, since the moral value appears to be in following a command of God or reflecting him/it as much as possible. Of course, this seems patently ridiculous. None of this plays well with our sense of moral intuition; moral intuition is wrong, or at least it is only right when it correctly reflects God's nature of commands. We feel we are being good by doing A for X and Y reason. And yet A is actually good *solely* because it is reflective of God. Yet most everybody being good on a practical daily basis believes X and Y rather than thinking of reflecting God in each and every instance of being good.

5. **Which God? Which commands?** – We are also unclear as to which god we are talking about, and what his/her/its commands are. The commands in the Old Testament appear to have been replaced overnight with the commands of the New Testament, at least for the Christian followers. Incidentally, this looks like moral relativism (something I call Inter-Testamental Moral Relativism) because the historical and geographic context of the Jews defined the morality of their actions. So there is a gross lack of clarity in what actions *do* reflect God's nature – we might call this the Argument From Divine Miscommunication. Is the stoning of adulterers good? Is it bad? Is it only good before 33 CE? Did God's nature change then? Is all the Bible literally true? If so, then Jesus is literally a door. If not, then Jesus and the Bible talk at times in metaphor. What is metaphor and what is literal? We do not

---

[1] As mentioned, perhaps "he" is more accurate than "it" here in the context of the Old Testament Yahweh god and the context being discussed.
[2] See how rape is countenanced in the Hebrew Bible, for example in Deuteronomy, in various contexts such as the spoils of war.

have commands for a good-many things in the Bible, what of these? Such divine commands are indeed muddled and unclear at best. Slavery (for example) appears to be morally bad, and yet God countenanced it in the Bible.

6. **Genocide and ordinary morality** – The idea that God commanded genocide in the Old Testament is also problematic and does not fit well with ordinary morality. But given DCT, it must be morally good. Or is it just good *sometimes?* This potentially gets you to an uncomfortable reality: DCT depends on who is doing or commanding it. Genocide from God = good. Genocide from Hitler = bad! It all starts looking like the context (moral relativism, again) and the consequences are all important. Hitler gets a lot of bad press for his terrible genocide. God less so. The scales are skewed, methinks.

7. **Is God a better stopping point?** – Theists have done nothing to show that God is a more appropriate stopping point than the moral properties of kindness, generosity and justice themselves. Why is it, in any rational sense, that grounding morality in God is actually any *better* than grounding it in real and observable features of the world, such as the consequences of moral actions? There seems to be this assumption that a framework set outside of our minds and our reality, dictated by some being that we cannot access or remotely understand, is somehow better.

8. **Why follow the commands?** – Why should we follow God's commands? Only to get into heaven and avoid hell? If so, then heaven and hell are consequential bribes to make one act morally. That is moral consequentialism, which gets in the way of acting truly altruistically. It's all about self-interest. Christians don't like to admit that. If this is so, that is not really a reason to be good. If it is because they are good things to do

based on moral reasoning, then again, the DCT framework fails because God does not have to provide a moral reason. In this way, there is no *reason* to accept DCT, even if it is true!

9. **Things not commanded are okay?** – Anything *not* commanded by God is potentially allowable. Since we cannot access the source directly (God), then we end up having to guess what is good or bad. This has to be a guess because it cannot be based on moral reasoning (because it has to be a divine command)! So anything not covered by divine commands in the Bible is potentially morally acceptable. Those actions lacking moral clarity leave us with either having to do moral reasoning, or simply not having a moral clue about what actions we should do in order to be reflective of God. This is even harder when it appears some things are both good and bad, depending on the context!

10. **But God would never command rape! Apart from he did.** – DCTers argue that God would never command bad things like murder and rape (i.e., that it is not in his nature). But this is falsified by the very fact that he *did* command them in the Bible! Including the death of all men, women, children and animals in different contexts. Some examples concerning rape in the Bible that have caused much debate: murder, rape, and pillage at Jabesh-gilead (Judges 21:10-24); murder, rape and pillage of the Midianites (Numbers 31:7-18); more Murder rape and pillage (Deuteronomy 20:10-14); laws of rape (Deuteronomy 22:28-29); death to the rape victim (Deuteronomy 22:23-24); David's punishment – polygamy, rape, baby killing, and God's "forgiveness" (2 Samuel 12:11-14); rape of female captives (Deuteronomy 21:10-14); rape and the spoils of war (Judges 5:30); sex slaves (Exodus 21:7-11); God assists rape and plunder (Zechariah 14:1-2). Nice.

11. **But God would never command rape! Er, how can you know?** – Again, the defence is common: "But God would *never* command rape!" Yet, in order to say that God would never command rape, we would have to know that rape is *already wrong*, independent of God! We cannot say God would never command it because it has never not commanded it (although see above), and to say that it wouldn't would involve moral reasoning, which is contrary to what the DCTers believe about God! We have this problem with causality, because the Christian can't say "We know he wouldn't command rape because we know it is bad because of X and Y reasons". Christian apologists get seriously hamstrung when they cannot appeal to moral reasoning!

12. **God cannot know it is itself all-good** – God cannot even know that it itself is all-good because to do so, it would need to judge itself on an objective standard! This is quite a difficult concept to think about, but how would God be able to have the self-reflective knowledge to be able to claim that it was all-good? All God could say was that it was Godlike. Good, being tautologous with God, means that God would work itself into a circle in trying to define itself. It is quite similar to God being unable to know that it is not a God-in-a-vat, and that there isn't a chain of gods, Matrix-style, above it.

13. **Moral development of children** – In *Morality Without God*, philosopher Walter Sinnott-Armstrong states:[1]

> ...anyone who helps and refrains from harming others just because God commanded her to do so might not be hard-hearted, but her motivations are far from ideal. It would be

---

[1] Sinnott-Armstrong, Walter (2011), *Morality Without God*, Oxford: Oxford University Press, p. 110.

better for them to help and refrain from harming other people out of concern for those other people.

That is what we ought to teach our children. Studies of development and education show that children develop better moral attitudes as adults if they are raised to empathise rather than to obey commands without any reasons in order to avoid punishment. To raise children to obey God's commands just because God commanded them will undermine true caring and true morality.

14. **Non-Christians who have no access to Christianity** – People who have not read the Bible or experienced the Christian God would have no idea how to be moral (unless there is an acceptable recourse to moral reasoning, which has no need of God). Think of ~~horrible people~~ horribly unlucky people existing before biblical times, or in different countries without access to those divine commands. Is murder then acceptable because they have not had divine commands?

Apologists like William Lane Craig have even posited ideas saying that God knew that these people would not freely come to love him, or would simply be bad people, so it front-loaded their souls into these pre-biblical times and places as cannon fodder.

15. **Stephen Maitzen: "Ordinary Morality Presupposes Atheism"** – Here is an argument from Stephen Maitzen (W. G. Clark Professor of Philosophy Chair, Research Ethics Board, Acadia University) to which we will return. This is an analogy used by Christians themselves. Imagine that you are a five-year-old being taken to the doctor for an injection against a deadly disease. You do not understand how immunisation works. Your parents cannot adequately explain it to you. You

just have to know that a greater good will come about from your immunisation. It is a piece of necessary pain and suffering, the needle going in, that will bring about a greater good. An onlooker would never, upon seeing the doctor about to inject this poor boy, run over and rugby tackle the doctor so as to stop the pain. That would stop the greater good from taking place. However, as illogical as this is, that *is* what every god-fearing Christian *should* do, given their moral system. Let me explain.

Imagine an old lady being set upon by some youths across the road. Using our ordinary morality, if we saw this, we would like to think we would step in and stop this from happening. But there can be no such thing as gratuitous evil in this world with an all-loving God, according to the Christian. This old woman getting beaten up, as horrible as it is, is necessary for a greater good to come about. By stepping in and helping this woman, we are stopping the greater good from coming about. If we were to stop those youths, it would be akin to rugby tackling the doctor to stop the pain, thus denying the greater good. In other words, as Maitzen states, ordinary morality simply does not make sense under theism. Ordinary morality presupposes atheism. Moreover, this whole scenario of the problem of evil and greater goods coming from suffering is *consequentialist* in nature. God is *using* people as a means to an end whereby the consequences of an action confer the moral value. This is the sort of utilitarianism that theists decry and attack atheists for holding to.

16. **God is a consequentialist** – And finally... A fundamental problem for Christians is that theologians claim that things like DCT are correct. But actually, most of the population tend to be consequentialists. As William Lane Craig has declared:

"consequentialism is a terrible ethic".[1] However, it turns out that about 90% of people are intuitively consequentialist. The most famous experiment to look into this is the trolley problem. This is where five people are working on a train track and there is a trolley hurtling towards them that will kill them. You can pull a lever to divert the trolley onto another track that will kill only a single worker. Do you pull the lever? It turns out that around 89% of people would pull the lever to save multiple people by killing one man. This goes dramatically down if they have to *push* a fat man off the bridge to block the trolley in his death (same calculation, but pushing a person directly rather than disconnectedly pulling a lever), which shows that morality is a function of psychology. It turns out that (as psychologist Jonathan Haidt would say in "The Emotional Dog and the Rational Tail"[2]) we intuitively moralise and then scrabble around for reasons as to why we did something. But Christians supposedly decry such consequentialism. This is rather interesting because (as we have seen) it turns out that God is the biggest consequentialist of them all. Theists argue that God moves in mysterious ways and that there is a reason for everything. Extending that logic, the Problem of Evil dictates that there can be no *gratuitous* evil in light of an all-loving god, that every bit of suffering must be necessary towards eventuating a greater good. So the moral value of the action that brings about suffering is in the consequence of the eventual greater good. It cannot be good in itself that all of the world, except the eight in Noah's family (and all of the animals bar a small number) died in a great

---

[1] As he did in his 2013 debate with physicist Laurence Krauss in Brisbane, Australia: "Life, the Universe, and Nothing (I): Has Science Buried God?". A transcript can be found online at https://www.reasonablefaith.org/media/debates/life-the-universe-and-nothing-i-has-science-buried-god (accessed 06/11/2021).
[2] Haidt, Jonathan (2001), "The emotional dog and its rational tail: a social intuitionist approach to moral judgment", *Psychological Review*, October 2001, 108(4): p. 814-34.

flood. No. So the goodness comes from the greater good that this brought about. Everything happens for a reason and God moves in mysterious ways. Jesus was sacrificed for the sins of the world. This was pure consequentialism. In fact, every atrocity in both the Bible and the real world is explained in this way. But, according to Christians, this ethic is terrible. The ethical system employed by theologians to use in *every single theodicy* is consequentialist. And apparently terrible!

That should really close the case on God being the objective basis of morality.

It seems clear to me from the above arguments that morality does not necessitate God, and that the notion of God grossly corrupts and complicates the idea of morality. Conversely, atheists have several very good cases for morality, which can take on many guises depending on what properties our reality has. It appears that morality and God are not good bedfellows; indeed, morality arguably requires atheism to make sense.

14 – Humans Do Not Have Free Will

Admittedly, I have discussed this in a previous section concerning God, and I will discuss it in a further section concerning heaven, but it will be useful to flesh out the idea somewhat here, too.

Arguments about free will, like anything in philosophy, depend rather a lot on definitions. For example, it turns out that I see myself as both a *determinist* and a *compatibilist* when it comes to free will, depending on the definition. Here, I will be using the following definition of free will:

> The real, rational and conscious ability to do otherwise in any given scenario, all things remaining equal.

In other words, this ability is derived both consciously and rationally. Further, an agent *really could* decide otherwise, as opposed to just theoretically having options. Free will sounds intuitively plausible, which is understandable given that most people who give the subject little thought would probably ascribe to such a working definition. Our inherited language and culture are littered with references to and belief in such a paradigm.

Let us look, though, at exactly what such a belief would entail, and why it fails. The above definition I will call libertarian free will (LFW), and the person who believes in it the libertarian free willer (LFWer).

For free will to make much sense at all, it needs to be grounded *rationally*. To say that one's choice to do an action is entirely irrational or a-rational (such as being random) is to deny any kind of sensible ownership of an action. In other words, it seems not to allow for the kind of responsibility people attach to freely willed decisions and resulting actions.

For example, let us take Wendy. She decides at 09:15 to give $5 to a homeless person she passes in the street. Now imagine that the world continues for any amount of time (say, ten minutes). We then rewind the world back to 09:15. The LFWer believes that Wendy, at 09:15, could just as well have decided *not* to have given the money to the homeless person, rationally and consciously even given that the entire world – every single variable contained therein – would have been identical (for it was the same world, ostensibly).

Let us concentrate on 09:15 to unpick this last point. This snapshot of time I will call the causal circumstance (CC). A causal circumstance is made up of, well, everything in the universe at that "snapshot". This would include, for any given person:

(1) Being born.
(2) Their genetic inheritance.
(3) Their life in the womb, shaping the genetic self.
(4) Their time and place of birth.
(5) Their parents, relatives, race and gender; the nurture and experiences in infancy and childhood.
(6) The mutations in their brain and body throughout life; and other purely random events.
(7) Their natural physical stature, looks, smile and voice; intelligence; sexual drive and proclivities; personality and wit; and natural ability in sports, music and dance.
(8) Their religious training; economic circumstances; cultural influences; political and civil rights; the prevailing customs of their times.
(9) The blizzard of experiences throughout life, not chosen by them but which happened to them. All the molecules, particles, forces and wave functions; i.e. the environment.

These things are in place, immovably so (since they are all variables that are inaccessible by being in some sense in the past, or instantaneously ungovernable) at the time of the decision making. In this causal circumstance (let's call it CC1), Wendy chooses to give the money away (let's call this A). So, in CC1, Wendy does A.

What this means is that Wendy's choice appears to be grounded in and is caused by all of those variables at play at that exact moment, CC1. The rational deliberative processes in her brain (the neurons and other neuro-structures) act upon those other variables (or are themselves acted upon by those variables) and the outcome is giving the money away.

Now let us return to this idea of continuing to live and then rewinding. This is a thought experiment. It does not matter whether we could, in actuality, rewind the clock. Perhaps quantum indeterminacy would get in the way, or Turing Problems, or some such idea. That is not relevant. What is relevant is that Wendy returns to this identical scenario, with the exact same causal circumstances (1) to (9) described above. Everything is the same. We have CC1 in every detail. However, this "second" time, the LFWer believes that Wendy could choose not to give the money away, or ~A (not A). This might look like a contravention of the Law of Non-Contradiction such that it is true that in CC1 Wendy does (or could do) A *and/or* ~A.

The real problem, though, is what would rationally ground this "second", different decision. Since everything in the universe, down to the rationalising processes and experiences in Wendy's brain would be identical, what possible reason could there be for Wendy choosing to do otherwise? What reason could there be that wasn't there "before"? What would cause a different weighing of factors in deliberation that wouldn't have manifested itself before?

When something happens, we should always ask *why*. In the case of an event involving an agent and their decisions, the LFWer usually gives up asking the why question when we get to the agent. But, as Schopenhauer once said, "A man can do what he wills, but he cannot will what he wills." This shows us that we should still keep asking the why question, especially of people's intentions and desires. And if there is an answer to these questions,a we invite some kind of causal determinism: effects have a cause, a reason, for being so. LFWers try to ground decisions in the *agent* and then give up looking for further causality, so that Wendy above would become like a miniature version of God, a Prime Mover, an Originator of a causal chain. Further, LFWers cannot have causality working *through* the agent, otherwise reasons for the agent's decision are not grounded (rationally and consciously) in *the agent* (i.e., *in Wendy*). In other words, Wendy chose to give the money away on her own, and her decision cannot defer to antecedent causality (i.e., God or external variables). This allows Wendy to be "morally responsible" for the action…supposedly. Usually, theologians and apologists only ascribe such prime mover skills to God (as can be seen in the Kalam Cosmological Argument [KCA]) and yet here they are, smuggling such origination into human beings every time they commit a freely willed action (indeed, LFW and the KCA are logically incompatible, though this might upset theistic apologists)!

Hopefully, you can clearly see the problems for LFW. For the LFWer, a decision in an agent needs to be grounded in the agent with no recourse to antecedent causality. The agent needs to be able to choose A or ~A in any given scenario. And they need to be able to do this with the entire universe being identical (simply the same causal circumstance), thus stripping any differential grounding away from the different decisions. This makes the reason for any difference in decision look rather like random. There is nothing that could *cause* the decision, nor would the LFWer *want there to be*.

And this is why it makes no sense as a logical position.

The remaining positions, then, are *determinism* (often called *hard determinism*) where the universe strictly adheres to cause and effect (or *adequate determinism* where it does on the macro-level but which has quantum indeterminacy at the micro-level) or *compatibilism* where determinism and free will are compatible with each other (compatibilism is sometimes called *soft determinism*). These positions (quantum aside) leave the agent unable to do otherwise. And this is where the equivocation comes in. Determinists deny LFW. It does not exist, so free will does not exist. Compatibilists deny LFW too. But they take the term *free will* and mould it into something new; they redefine it. Compatibilists usually define free will as:

> The ability to consciously and rationally do that which one desires.

Of course, that which one desires will itself be determined, but there is a sense of the agent being the *author* and *owner* of their actions. It is worth reminding ourselves here that quantum indeterminacy is no bedfellow to this understanding of free will. Specifically, if some of the variables involved in a decision are random, an agent cannot be said to have rational or conscious control over that decision (which is why there is a more recent move to label free will deniers as hard *incompatibilists* rather than *hard determinists*).

This is, however, just the philosophical side of the argument. I could bring in any number of scientific, biological, genetic, psychological, and behavioural data to defend these claims. Humans are, it seems, pretty predictable, despite how unique we like to claim we are. Check out my chapter on free will in John Loftus's *Christianity in the Light of Science* for more on this.[1]

Calvinists (members of a particular denomination of Christianity) offer themselves to be the odd ones out, certainly in the Christian cloisters of world religion. They are deterministic, believing that humans have no free will and everything happens at the predetermined behest of God. Almost all other Christians disagree because they view God as judgemental, with the carrot of heaven or stick of hell being the bribing consequences. For such retributive punishment systems to make any sense, with the notion of *just deserts* driving the punitive cogs, humans have to have the real and actual ability to do otherwise. If this

---

[1] "Free Will" in Loftus, John (2016), *Christianity in the Light of Science*, Amherst: Prometheus Books.

is not the case, then God simply creates people to be condemned to an eternity in hell or rewarded with an eternity in paradise without being able to effect a change to those outcomes.

You could argue that Calvinists make more sense of earthly reality than most other theists.

Exactly how does it work that God can be knowledgeable of every single potential counterfactual (i.e., an "if statement" regarding what might happen in a given scenario) in theoretical or actual reality, and yet I still have free will to do otherwise? In other words, if God knows that I am going to make a cup of tea at 10:15 on Tuesday morning, then how could I *actually* choose to do otherwise? Some theists claim that just because God knows this eventuality, doesn't mean to say it *causes* it, it just *knows* my freely willed decision. Okay, let's grant that. But this is not quite the point. If I am infallibly, indubitably going to make that cup of tea at that time, then in what possible way am I *able* to do otherwise? The LFWer, as defined, believes I really *can* do A and ~A, but such divine foreknowledge means I can only fulfil one option at the expense of being able to do any other.

Therefore, we are left with a concept of free will (this contra-causal, libertarian notion) that makes no sense in philosophical and theological contexts, and that is not supported by any evidence. Without this concept, most conceptions of God (for example, the Christian OmniGod) are thoroughly incoherent. God's judgement, and heaven and hell as eternal reward and punishment, are rendered nonsensical when seen in the context of people living in a universe without libertarian free will. And yet neither God nor humanity have this form of free will. And without this keystone, this fundamental brick, the edifice of judgemental OmniGod theism comes tumbling down.

15 – The Bible Is Not a Good Source of Morality

Of course, you could make many of the same arguments against any other holy book that has ever been written, I'm sure. I am being, again, Christo-centric here by admission. I'm sorry not sorry.

Before we get onto the topic at hand, let us remind ourselves for a short while of *deontology* (objective morality).

Deontology is a moral framework famously championed by Immanuel Kant. Deontologists believe that there are things that we categorically should do, things that ought to be done irrespective of the context. No matter how good the effects of an action might appear, the action might still be bad. Kant, as the deontological flag-bearer, argued there were moral laws and prohibitions that ought to be adhered to, regardless of the consequences, and that people should not be used as a means to an end.

Imagine again a scenario where someone needs to be saved. A deontologist would act according to a rule such as Kant's Categorical Imperative: "Act only according to that maxim whereby you can, at the same time, will that it should become a universal law."[1] Saving others could be willed as a universal law and we should do it, unconditionally, as an end in itself.

Let's apply deontology, then, to the Bible and Christianity:

---

[1] Kant, Immanuel (1993), *Grounding for the Metaphysics of Morals*, trans. Ellington, James W., 3rd ed., Indianapolis: Hackett, p. 30.

- It is wrong to commit genocide. But God and Yahwists did it, e.g., 1 Samuel 15; Exodus 17.
- It is wrong to lie. But God did, certainly by proxy, e.g., 1 Kings 22:23; Jeremiah 4:10; 2 Thessalonians 2:11; and others.
- It is wrong to rape. But God sanctioned it, e.g., Judges 21; Numbers 31; Deuteronomy 20, 21, 22 etc.
- It is wrong to own slaves. But God allowed for it, e.g., Leviticus 25; Exodus 21 etc.

And so on. You get the point.

Applying a (deontological and arguably absolutist) moral framework that Bible believers use (and this can include all those of the Abrahamic faiths) – deontological and absolutist – to the Bible itself can cause great logical discomfort to those believers!

I will furnish you with some further Hebrew Bible moral lessons.

Noah's Flood – mass murder is okay if you've messed up your project. When things get tough, don't bother trying to change people, just give up and start again by drowning all the people and all the animals, apart from a few.

Mutilating a penis can change God's mind. God was about to kill Moses until Zipporah, his wife, took a flint and cut off her son's foreskin and touched Moses' feet with it. This caused God to "let Moses alone". (Exodus 4: 24-26)

Slavery's fine, just don't treat them *too* badly. Yes, at no point is slavery outlawed or condemned in the Bible, even by Jesus. In fact, it is countenanced. If you kill a slave from beating them too much, you will be punished, but "if the slave survives a day or two, there shall be no punishment; for the slave is the owner's property". (Exodus 21:20-21)

Homosexual activity deserves death. Oh dear. (Leviticus 20:13)

Victims of rape must marry their rapists. If a man comes across a virgin who is not betrothed and rapes her, and they are discovered, the rapist must pay the father of the victim some money, and then marry her "for he has violated her". (Deuteronomy 22:28-29)

It's okay to test someone's loyalty by making them almost kill their own son. The story of Abraham and Isaac is morally abhorrent. God, incredibly powerful and awesome, orders Abraham to sacrifice his son as a burnt offering to show his fealty. Just as Abraham is about to kill his beloved child, God's angel intervenes and stops him, providing a ram instead. Close shave. Abusive.[1]

God loves to kill children and animals by the nation-load. The Exodus account is a funny one. And by "funny", I mean absolutely morally disgusting. Because the Pharaoh refuses to let the Hebrew people go – because God itself has hardened his heart! – God sends down a number of plagues to wreak havoc on ~~the Pharaoh~~ the men, women, children and animals of the whole nation of Egypt.

The plagues are water turning to blood, frogs, lice, flies, livestock pestilence, boils, hail, locusts, darkness and the killing of firstborn children. Honestly, actually consider that God enacted these punishments on the entire Egyptian people, as though they could all be culpable for the Pharaoh's decision and all be evil enough to deserve torture and death. And remember this was the torture and death of animals and children, too.

Genocide. God is love. Nothing represents the pure, unfiltered love of God for all of its creation like ~~killing billions of organisms in a flood. Or slavery. Or killing gays. Or making women marry their rapists.~~ genocide. Take your pick in the Bible: Deuteronomy 7:1-6 or 20:10-19 for starters. Or there is this lovely passage (from Numbers 31:1-18):

> "Have you allowed all the women to live?" he asked them.
> "They were the ones who followed Balaam's advice and were

---

[1] There are actually rabbinic traditions in which the sacrifice of Isaac was carried out, and God raised Isaac from death and restored him to Abraham as a reward for his faithfulness. Some have suggested that these retain a memory of an alternative version of this story from the distant past and a time when human sacrifice to Yahweh was deemed as acceptable, if not commendable.

101

the means of turning the Israelites away from the LORD in what happened at Peor, so that a plague struck the LORD's people. Now kill all the boys. And kill every woman who has slept with a man, but save for yourselves every girl who has never slept with a man."

What this holy book seems to be teaching us is that violence and death are the answer to pretty much everything (along with some other very dubious lessons).

These represent just a tiny selection of what could be taken and exemplified from within the Hebrew Bible.

Let me take some time to be a bit more Christo-centric in quoting some of the truly problematic things that the New Testament Gospel writers claimed Jesus said. Here are a number of problematic Jesus quotes. This first is from Luke 14:

> 26 "If anyone comes to Me and does not hate his own father, mother, wife, children, brothers, sisters, yes, and even his own life, he cannot be My disciple. 27 Whoever does not carry his own cross and come after Me cannot be My disciple.

Author and former minister David Madison (PhD Biblical Studies) points out in his analysis of this quote in his book *Ten Things Christians Wish Jesus Hadn't Taught*,[1] imagine if a modern religious leader said this. What would people think? Precisely what I think when I read the above. No divided loyalties, your cult comes first.

This is about cult loyalty.

I wonder how many Christians really follow the words of God, in incarnated human form (Luke 14):

> 33 So then, none of you can be My disciple who does not give up all his own possessions.

---

[1] Madison refers here to the late biblical scholar Hector Avalos who makes the same point in his book *The Bad Jesus*.

I am not sure how you can adhere to the "Prosperity Gospel", whereby pastors have a number of private jets and gazillions of dollars, when you read the words of God like this. I bet Joel Osteen doesn't have this as his Sunday reading.

Divorce is fairly common these days, representing around 50% of marriages. Jesus in Mark 10 says:

> 11 And He said to them, "Whoever divorces his wife and marries another woman commits adultery against her; 12 and if she herself divorces her husband and marries another man, she is committing adultery."

A very problematic quote from Jesus sees him not wanting everyone to access his words and repentance. As Mark 4 states:

> 10 As soon as He was alone, His followers, along with the twelve disciples, began asking Him about the parables. 11 And He was saying to them, "To you has been given the mystery of the kingdom of God, but for those who are outside, everything comes in parables, 12 so that while seeing they may see, and not perceive, and while hearing, they may hear, and not understand, otherwise they might return and it would be forgiven them."

The ramifications of not accessing the truth and not believing are very clear, as the Gospel of John elucidates (John 3):

> 18 The one who believes in Him is not judged; the one who does not believe has been judged already, because he has not believed in the name of the only Son of God....
>
> 36 The one who believes in the Son has eternal life; but the one who does not obey the Son will not see life, but the wrath of God remains on him."

God appears to be holding revelation from some people and then punishing them on account of their not believing.

I have given you but the smallest of tastes of what the Bible contains. There is so much more; luckily, there are whole books written on the moral problems of the Bible, and I suggest you read around on the subject. Thankfully, in modern times, we have done a much better job of morality in documents like the UN Charter of Human Rights. Such documents involve the use of modern, enlightened moral reasoning.

Christian apologists claim to adhere to some form of deontology and yet this kind of moral *absolutism* causes moral *mayhem* for them when looking at the Bible. That said, I am not a fan of deontology – and this larger idea of moral realism – and I *do* think it is a hard system to defend for a naturalist (well, for anyone). But when defended by the theist – the Christian, here (for the New Testament, though Jews and Muslims as well for the Hebrew Bible) – it appears to be a case of referring back to a 2,000-year-old book for absolutist laws that make no sense now.

Times have changed. Genocide's not so cool anymore. Dashing babies' heads on rocks is frowned upon. Slavery, unless you are waving a flag at an American political insurrection, is generally considered poor form.[1]

What we do these days is correct:

(1) Do moral reasoning first.
(2) *Then* appraise ancient books for their moral value based on our moral reasoning.

What we shouldn't do, but a surprising number of people still do, is as follows:

---

[1] Deliberate understatement. Of course I mean morally abhorrent!

(1) Assume the moral genius of a very old, parochial, patriarchal book.

(2) Spend the rest of our lives mentally contorting and gerrymandering to square those absolute moral claims and lessons with our modern moral reasoning.

It's an impossible task, but it doesn't stop people from trying.

16 – What Holy Books Forgot to Say...

I have given you a little hint of what in this case the Hebrew Bible (or Old Testament) and the New Testament say in terms of delivering moral(ly abhorrent) lessons. This pertains to a good proportion of the world's population (Christians, Muslims, and Jews).

The previous argument addressed what these holy books say. Often, however, the problem is not what the holy books *say*, but what they *don't say*.

In the following discussion, I will be exemplifying the problems here in the context of the Bible, but you can apply them to many other holy books, such as the Qu'ran.

Many holy books claim to include prophecy. And many holy books concern themselves with either divine figures or people who have preferential access to divine figures. Let's take any of the Hebrew Bible prophets, such as Isaiah, Ezekiel, and Daniel (considered a prophet in Christianity). We will have to park the fact that most modern scholars now accept that these authors or redactors wrote or compiled *ex eventu*, which is to say they actually wrote *after* the events they supposedly prophesied and *then* dated their work (or had it dated) back to before the events. This is an uncomfortable truth; however, let's ignore that and assume that these seers really were prophets.

My complaint here is that these prophets, with their nebulous predictions, tell us next to nothing.

I mean, really, nothing. Nothing of use, at any rate.

Isn't it suspicious that none of them predicted cars, aircraft, space travel, inter-continental ballistic missiles, germ theory, and more? There is so much they *didn't* predict that they *could have* and it would have been morally ground-breaking, potentially saving umpteen millions of lives.

Instead, they predicted events that really were conspicuously contextual and unimaginative. Indeed, precisely what you would expect if you were writing *ex eventu* prophecies.

And the same goes for the headliner figures like Jesus and Muhammad. That they didn't say certain things ends up being a very strong argument against the truth of who they or others said they were. No god or divine figure or prophet (who could bend the ear of a god) would be so absent-minded as to forget to say that slavery really was bad, or that you should boil medical tools and water, or that germs work in a given particular way, or this, or that. You really could think of a very long list of things such prominent religious luminaries *should have said*. This is a morally problematic scenario.

Slavery is a particularly interesting example because the Bible was so ambiguous concerning (or, more accurately, supportive of) it. Accordingly, the Bible was used to justify slavery in the Antebellum South in the US. This would never have happened if the Bible had been clear on the matter, if it had unambiguously condemned the system. But, instead, it countenances it (e.g. Leviticus 25:44-46; Numbers 31; Ephesians 6:5; the Covenant Code; and so on).

These religious figures not only *supposedly said* incredibly morally dubious things but also *didn't say* incredibly morally good things. Therefore, the Bible is a good argument against the existence of OmniGod from both directions.

It could have been a book chock-full of brilliant advice and knowledge that would have saved so much pain and suffering – both from moral instruction and scientific or knowledge-based instruction. And yet tumbleweed.

Jonathan MS Pearce

Part Four

THE PROBLEM OF EVIL

No discussion about God's existence is complete without discussing the *problem of evil*. It is a mainstay in theological wrangles and has to be the biggest ~~thorn~~ spear in the side of theists in terms of arguments against the existence of God, primarily because of its emotive appeal.

The argument is as follows. There is pain and suffering in this world. For this, on top of obvious pains and sufferings, we can add all sorts of ideas like anxiety, fear, terror, and other psychological ills. Given that God is omniscient, it should *know* what to do about it; given that God is omnipotent, it should be *able* to do something about it; and given that God is omnibenevolent, it should *care* enough to *want* to do something about it. So what gives?

What gives is either God does not exist, or God is not OmniGod (but some lesser iteration of a divine being), or there is a reason for the pain and suffering we see that excuses OmniGod. Usually, this involves arguing that there is a greater good that comes about as a result of it.

This is an age-old problem, and theists have been defending their position of believing in an OmniGod in light of obvious suffering on Earth for thousands of years. These defensive moves are called *theodicies*. Some philosophers have suggested that theodicies are *themselves* immoral or even evil, since they are attempts to morally justify wholly horrific events.

This is worth dwelling on for a short while. It might depend how you do your morality, but it appears (as already mentioned in a previous argument) that theodicies work using *consequentialist ethics* – the goodness of an action is derived from the outcomes that are obtained from the action. Theists generally hate this moral framework because it has no need for God to work, and so they reject it. But then use it. All of the time. Theodicies excuse evils on account of those evils obtaining greater goods. I have argued elsewhere that God is a consequentialist, including in my last book *Why I Am Atheist and Not a Theist: How To Do Knowledge, Morality, and Meaning in a Godless World*. At the very least, God is using people instrumentally to obtain a greater good, and excusing evil and suffering in achieving certain objectives. In some sense, God cannot be *all*-good or *all*-loving if it allows or necessitates some (arguably a great deal of) evil to obtain a greater good. To refer to Dan Barker again:[1]

> The combination of omnipotence, omniscience and omnibenevolence is what makes the Problem of Evil such a thorn to traditional theists. Although technically the Problem of Evil is not an incoherency argument–the existence of evil is positive empirical evidence against the existence of an all-good deity–it is the "omni" in omnibenevolence that makes it incompatible with omniscience. If God knows in advance that there will be evil as a direct or indirect result of his actions, then he is not all good. He is at least partly responsible for the harm. Since God has the desire and the power to eliminate evil, why doesn't he?

Over time, two versions of the argument have arisen: the *logical* problem of evil and the *evidential* problem of evil.

The logical problem of evil (that OmniGod and suffering are logically incompatible) is answered by theists in an appeal to *skeptical theism*. God moves in mysterious ways – we don't or cannot know the mind of God. The theist defends the existence of suffering in the context of an all-loving god by claiming that there is no *logical*

---

[1] Barker, Dan (2008), *Godless*, Berkeley, CA: Ulysses Press, p. 126.

impossibility or contradiction in suffering *and* OmniGod existing. There *could* be a reason why such suffering exists. It *might* be that to have goodness necessitates having evil, or that suffering builds the soul, or that it is a necessary corollary of free will, or…or…

There are lots of coulds and ifs and maybes and mights that are best summed up by God having some reason, but we're not wholly sure what the reasons definitely are.

This is arguably the *possibiliter ergo probabiliter* fallacy whereby the theist sees a logical *possibility* and then jumps from possibility to certainty. "Well it *might* be the case, so therefore it *is* the case."

Technically, they can get away with this: there is no logical impossibility in suffering existing as well as an OmniGod existing. There *could* be a reason why 230,000 people and countless animals had to die in the 2004 tsunami. Sure. I mean, unicorns *could* exist. But do they? Is it probable that they do?

The problem with the logical problem of evil can be seen when we do a *reductio ad absurdum* – when we take the thought experiment to its absurd extremes to highlight certain qualities of the argument. In this case, imagine the following "absurd" scenario. You are the last person left on Earth. All other humans, including all of your family members, have been tortured over decades by God. All other animals as well. It has been a truly horrific time, and you have witnessed the worst things imaginable, committed by God. This is now the fiftieth year of terrible torture for you, on your own.

And yet you can *still* claim that there might be a greater good, unbeknownst to you, as to why this state of affairs is taking place in light of God *still* being perfect. It is not logically impossible that God is still omnibenevolent – still an all-loving entity – in light of such a huge amount of suffering. You have no idea what the reasoning is, and it seems absolutely preposterous to claim that God is all-loving when witnessing and *experiencing* these things. But it *could* be the case.

In fact, as mentioned in a previous design argument, the theist in such a terrible situation *could* (and indeed would *have to*) argue that such a terrible world of torture would still be the perfect creation.

That is a ridiculous argument, but it is the hypothetical destination at which an obedient theist must find themselves if they follow the logic.

So then we get onto the second formulation of the problem of evil: the *evidential* problem of evil. This is to accept that the logical problem may be "answered" by OmniGod *possibly* having a reason to allow or even cause such suffering (that it provides a greater good). But the amount or type of suffering acts as evidence *against* the existence of OmniGod. We move from an argument of *logical contradiction* to one of *probability*.

Take the torture scenario above. All of that torture and pain and death that *appears* morally abhorrent in light of OmniGod does, indeed, constitute evidence that God is either not omnibenevolent or does not exist. It all lowers the probability of OmniGod existing. So whilst OmniGod is not logically *impossible*, it ends up being *incredibly improbable*.

As we discussed in the argument about this being a perfect world, the theist has to look at every single piece of suffering and argue that it is *necessary* for a greater good to come about, such that each successive unit of pain (and sometimes, more problematically, the smaller units of pain like a stubbed toe) becomes a greater stretch for the defence. On the other hand, the atheist sees each successive unit of pain as further evidence against the existence of OmniGod.

And since there can be no unnecessary suffering, this might also lead to moral paralysis. This is something discussed by philosopher Stephen Maitzen in his paper "Ordinary Morality Implies Atheism", as mentioned in the divine command theory chapter.

I will present a little more meat to the bone here.

What Maitzen suggests is that we start with something he calls *theological individualism* (TI), defined as "Necessarily, God permits undeserved, involuntary human suffering only if such suffering ultimately produces a net benefit for the sufferer".[1] If this is the case, then, by stopping suffering, we are stopping the necessary greater good

---

[1] Maitzen, Stephen (2009), "Ordinary Morality Implies Atheism", *European Journal for Philosophy of Religion*, 2, p. 108.

coming about from the instance of suffering. An example might be this: If a doctor is giving a child a vaccine, we might see that vaccine injection as an instance of suffering. Therefore, we should intervene and stop the pain for the child. But in doing this, we would be stopping the good that would come out of it. In this case, we would be stopping the immunity to a given disease such that the child might die.

Theologically speaking, all instances of suffering will necessarily beget a greater good because there simply *can be no gratuitous suffering*, and so we should allow all suffering to take place. This is incredibly counter-intuitive and morally problematic. Our ordinary sense of morality means that we would of course want to step in and stop an old lady from being beaten up and mugged on the other side of the road. But by helping her out, we are denying the necessary good that would come about from the event had we not stepped in! Therein lies a problem with such theistic morality because it seems to suggest that there must necessarily be a greater good for all suffering, and this can produce problems.

You can argue that this greater good in such a situation is for the person themselves such that the old lady is getting beaten up, but that the greater good must come to *her* in some way necessarily. On the other hand, maybe the greater good is for someone else. But then the old lady is being used instrumentally to obtain a greater consequence for someone other than her. This is even more problematic for most theists as this is classic utilitarianism that looks no different from murdering someone who walks into a hospital in order to harvest their organs to allow five *other* people to survive.

Furthermore, you cannot use an eternal paradise in heaven for the old lady as a defence because this is *compensation* and not *moral justification*. Again, compensation used to morally justify something can only be used in moral consequentialism, a moral value theory that most theists abhor. If I punch you in the face and break your jaw because I don't like the look of your face, then the court might make me pay you $10,000 as compensation. But this does not make the original punching you in the face a *good* moral action. Only a larger-view consequentialism can get something approaching this, with some caveats.

In other words, for the old lady getting mugged, theistic morality should cause us to be morally paralysed, allowing all evils and suffering to take place in order to release the greater good that *has to* come about because OmniGod cannot allow gratuitous suffering. We should not step in to stop her getting mugged because moral paralysis will allow the greater good that would be necessary to come to fruition!

As a note to explain why there are only two arguments in this problem of evil section, due to the connected nature of all of these topics, several of the problem of evil arguments are filed under other sections (the abortion and perfect world arguments to name a few). Nevertheless, here are a few more for you, on top of what you have undoubtedly just enjoyed.

Also, don't let the theist try on the *tu quoque* fallacy in claiming that we have no right to talk about suffering and evil. They might say that, somehow, without God, atheists can't make sense of evil and suffering. *Tu quoque* means "you too" in the sense of the following. Imagine I caught Carla stealing a car and accused her of this moral wrong, and she rebuked me, saying, "Yeah, but *you* stole a car last week". Although I may have been hypocritical, it does not excuse her own moral misdemeanour or explain it. Likewise, it is irrelevant whether atheists can or can't explain suffering, evil, and morality from within their own worldview (we can). The theist here is still left defending the problem of evil.

When an atheist accuses the theist's god of being morally bad or incomprehensible, it is not good enough for the theist to rebuke the atheist for their own moral worldview. It is a distraction and fallacious.

17 – Natural Evil Shows God's Shadier Side

As I have detailed, theistic answers – theodicies – for the problem of evil revolve around appeals to God having some unknown or guessed-at reason for creating or allowing such evil or suffering to exist in the world. So there is a logical get-out-of-jail free card that does less for the theist than they think it does. After all, unicorns *could* exist.

But they don't.

Let me explain.

Theists try to get God off the hook by blaming humans. God created humans, but there is also evil in the world. God cannot be evil and cannot create suffering in the way it certainly looks like it has, so it has to be someone else's fault. It's those pesky humans. But they conveniently forget that God designed and created those pesky humans knowingly – everything is contingent upon God, theists claim (including evil, I claim). So theodicies usually explain away evil in terms of human behaviour or the human journey. Here are some common examples of theodicies:

- Free will means that humans have the freedom to choose to do both good and bad things. Free will is super important, making it worth all the suffering that comes from (human-caused) freely chosen murder, rape, and genocide that comes from having it. Bad choices and moral mayhem are the collateral of free will.

- The Original Sin situation – we are all being punished for the sins of Adam and Eve (as previously discussed). This means that we are still suffering as a result of The Fall, and Adam and Eve's decision.

- The soul-making theodicy posits that we are unfinished creations. We are on a journey of building up our souls, and suffering in the world enables us to become better people. Or souls. Or something.

- You can't have warm without cold, or good without evil. So suffering has to exist in order for moral goodness to exist.

- The perfect world theodicy is one previously discussed in the design section. This is somehow the optimal or perfect amount of pain and suffering.

There are others, and it is worth noting that theists often use them in conjunction with each other.

These theodicies struggle to really account for the huge events of evil and suffering like 6 million Jews dying in a Holocaust, other genocides, wars and so on. Could we still have achieved God's objectives with fewer Jews dying? How about two fewer?[1] Would two fewer Jews dying not have brought about the same outcomes? Is this not a case of God using those people as a means to an end, so God is using the Jews instrumentally to achieve some greater good? Is this the kind of morality that theists espouse?

So on and so forth.

But one thing that isn't really touched by these theodicies is natural evil. This is defined as suffering caused by earthquakes, tsunamis, natural forest fires, and other such natural events that cause untold harms, often to the animal world outside of humanity. A fawn dying in a forest fire after days of terrible suffering and burns, unbeknownst to humanity, has nothing to do with our free will, is very

---

[1] Theists sometimes argue that you can keep saying this until you get to zero, and thus the criticism is invalidated. But applying this in reverse means that, on the flipside, this present/historical amount of suffering *has* to be the optimal amount.

difficult to justify with Original Sin, and makes little sense in light of the usual theodicies.

These natural evils seem to be more obviously unnecessary and more difficult to explain in light of OmniGod.

Surely, with these sorts of natural evils, a good god would want to stop the suffering (and could stop it), yet it appears that the unnecessary sufferings still exist. Fawns still burn in forest fires.

Undaunted, the theist can still posit that there *might be* a greater good or a good reason for such natural evil to exist, though they cannot easily appeal to any human-centric theodicy. I do think that natural evil makes it *even more* difficult to cook up some theodicy to try to get God off the hook.

Animal suffering, as a result, is seen by many thinkers as the strongest challenge to the defence of the problem of evil. Here is an example of such an argument that could be formulated:[1]

(1) God is omnipotent, omniscient and wholly good.
(2) The evil of extensive animal suffering exists.
(3) Necessarily, God can actualise an evolutionarily perfect world.
(4) Necessarily, God can actualise an evolutionarily perfect world only if God does actualise an evolutionarily perfect world.
(5) Necessarily, God actualised an evolutionarily perfect world.

(5) follows from (3) and (4), but we have a contradiction since (5) and (2) cannot both be true. So it appears that (1) is false.

The argument is to say that God could predict the mechanisms of evolution and design one in which animal suffering is minimised. This scenario can be called an "evolutionarily perfect world". We could imagine a scenario where God could put in place an evolutionary system whereby (for example) just before a gazelle is given a killing bite by a lion, a gene is expressed that naturally tranquilises the gazelle. Or some such similar situation. But this appears *not* to be the case. Instead,

---

[1] Adapted from Michael Almeida's Darwinian Problem of Evil in his 2012 book *Freedom, God, and Worlds*, Oxford: OUP, p. 194-95.

we have extensive animal suffering that is hard-baked into the evolutionary system and world.

Indeed, this is a more formal iteration of the previous argument in the book about photosynthesis and why there is carnivorousness at all.

Whether it is carnivorousness, animal disease, plate tectonics, forest fires, or any other natural evil, it all needs to be explained in terms of OmniGod. But in the same way that I don't believe in unicorns merely *because they are logically possible*, I don't believe that OmniGod exists in light "of suffering over three billion years of evolutionary carnage"[1] *merely because such a scenario is logically possible.*

The main thrust of this argument, then, is not only does suffering need to be explained in light of OmniGod, but the huge suffering of creatures (not humans) needs to be explained in terms of OmniGod (and not humans). It's bad enough that animals suffer when they don't have to, but it's quite another to say that their suffering is the fault of humans as if they have to pay the price for our choices in the context of God's design.

But if we're not to blame, then who is?

It's not hard to guess.

---

[1] Ibid., p. 194.

18 – Where Is God Hiding?

Since you've been away on holiday
We've stomached your archaic rule
And since you've been away on holiday
We've hosted some wars over you
So stay away on holiday, my friend, we don't need your
services
Your excuses, your mysterious ways...
What a mysterious way to behave
What a mysterious way to just go away

Lord, let us go

I've always liked the lyrics of a band called Cursive, whose album *Happy Hollow* is very much about skepticism of God's existence. The above words are taken from their song "Retreat!", a song that takes a dig at God's absence.

Because it really does look like God has been away on holiday for a few thousand years, but no one knows where, and it has left no contact details. In the context of Judeo-Christianity, God was all involved in the world's affairs, interfering here, getting in waist-deep there, turning someone into a pillar of salt here, causing a flood there. And then, suddenly, *poof!* It was gone.

Rather coincidentally, in the modern age of video cameras and live recording, God really is absent. No miracles, no nothing.

You might wonder why this argument appears in the Problem of Evil section rather than the Why We Believe (Or Not) section. It could qualify for either, but the reality is that anything to do with unfairness (as some of those previous sections have been) can be seen in light of suffering or evil in the world. And such negative scenarios need to be understood in terms of OmniGod. This is the problem of evil in another guise, and such counter-arguments are, again, theodicies.

This argument is called the Divine Hiddenness Argument. The formalised version of it (as espoused by philosophers J.L. Schellenberg, Stephen Maitzen, and Jason Marsh) is somewhat more technical and nuanced than what is presented here, which is much more connected to the two previous arguments concerning the unfair amount of evidence, and the distribution of belief around the world. The idea is that there are nonbelievers who are perfectly capable of having a loving relationship with God but don't because of where and when they were born, and the lack of feasible access to Godly evidence. We discussed these people earlier in the book as *nonresistant nonbelivers*. God, for them, remains hidden over time and place.

This is how the argument looks:

(1) If there is a God, he is perfectly loving.
(2) If a perfectly loving God exists, there are no nonresistant nonbelievers.
(3) There are and often have been nonresistant nonbelievers.
(4) No perfectly loving God exists.
(5) There is no God.

Another such form might be:

(1) God has allowed himself to remain hidden from many people.
(2) It would be bad for an omnipotent, omniscient God to remain hidden (or to keep his reasons for being hidden) from anyone.
(3) God, being perfectly good, cannot do anything that is bad.
(4) Therefore, there is no God.

This is a very effective argument that has warranted an awful lot of ink to be spilt over it. But we will concentrate more in this chapter on the absence of God in a more particular way.

A personal God seems to have arisen as an idea in conjunction with agriculture, about 10,000–12,000 years ago. This means that for the first 190,000 years of God's existence, it really was absent. But even since the development of ideas of monotheism – a single god like the OmniGod we are discussing – those who do believe frequently experience doubts, unrewarding prayers and rituals, spiritual dryness, or downright catastrophes taking place where God seems absent or non-responsive. The idea here is that God is not only hidden to Amazonian tribespeople who have no hope of accessing whatever version of it might be true from contexts outside of the great rainforest, but that God is also absent to those involved with any given religious movement.

In this way, God's absence is particularly felt when *believers* are suffering. The feeling of divine absence is thus itself a form of suffering. This is really well articulated by philosopher Ian DeWeese-Boyd:[1]

> Accordingly, those who experience divine absence feel their flourishing destroyed and hopes dashed, because they have identified their flourishing with God's presence and hoped that God would alleviate their suffering, or, at least, accompany them in it. Their question is not how suffering is conceptually compatible with a God of love, rather it is more in line with the cries of the psalmist, "Why hast thou forsaken me?" (Ps. 22:1) or "Why standest thou afar off, O Lord? why hidest thou thyself in times of trouble?" (Ps. 10:1). For those suffering in this way, no merely theoretical explanation will suffice. As Howard-Snyder and Moser note, answers to this existential problem "often seem lame, if not contrived,"

---

[1] From his excellent chapter "Lyric theodicy : Gerard Manley Hopkins and the problem of existential hiddenness" in Green, Adam and Stump, Eleanore (2015), *Hidden Divinity and Religious Belief*, Cambridge: Cambridge University Press, p. 262.

leading in some cases to "further frustration, and eventually to bitterness and despair."[1] Conceptual answers in such a situation are sand to the thirsty and stone to those who hunger for bread.

In DeWeese-Boyd's chapter, he looks at how poet Gerard Manley Hopkins struggled with the coexistence of faith and suffering, being unable to clearly explain the two with theodicy. "In this way, Hopkins's poetry raises theodicean questions, but, offering no clear, discursive answer to them, implies that theodicy, if available at all, may well leave us stumbling in the night."[2] The idea for the poet is that we often stand in darkness with only a too small and distant star of hope, but no real light to aid us. Indeed, Hopkins "consistently represents theodicy as either unattainable or impotent in the face of the suffering he experiences."[3]

Let us consider the "lamentations" – a prominent ancient literary genre – that we see in the Psalms and the Book of Lamentations in the Hebrew Bible. Here we see various versions of this grappling with why God would abandon and forsake such a chosen believer or nation. And, rather oddly, Jesus does this himself at the cross, lamenting why God had forsaken *him* (even though he was, theoretically, God).

Except, I would argue, the Gospel writers at the time (those before John) didn't see Jesus as God but as a divine Messiah-figure. Thus Jesus could quite easily say this and it would make sense. But if Jesus *is actually God in human form* (as the author of the Gospel of John seems to argue), then Jesus crying out to himself to lament why he has forsaken himself requires some theological wrangling. Of course, it is best understood by the fact that it never happened, and that the early Gospel writers were creating a narrative around their understanding of Jesus as a Messiah.

---

[1] Howard-Snyder , D. and Moser , P. K. (2002), *Divine Hiddenness: New Essays*, Cambridge: Cambridge University Press, p. 3.
[2] Green & Stump (2015), p. 264.
[3] Ibid., p. 265.

Yet again. I digress.

Yugin Nagasawa, in the aforementioned book, has his own chapter on divine hiddenness in a different context. He describes how secret Christians in 17th-century Japan were persecuted, illustrating a painful absence of God. They apparently received no assistance in their painful journey into martyrdom. There was no divine interference in the world at those moments in the way that God supposedly interfered for the merest of reasons in the Hebrew Bible. For the skeptic, this is obvious. God doesn't exist and the Hebrew Bible is largely mythological, being a legendary embellishment of a couple of historical kernels (or often outright fabrication) in order to provide a handbook of national identity whilst those who came to be known as the Jewish people were in exile in Babylonia. But if you believe it to be literally true, then you have to explain God's interference in one geographical and historical context and its abject absence in every other.

Nagasawa rightly sees this as a particularly acute problem:[1]

> I believe that the problem of divine absence constitutes one of the greatest challenges for theists because it involves (i) horrendous evil as opposed to ordinary evil; (ii) divine hiddenness from devout believers as opposed to divine hiddenness from ordinary believers or nonbelievers; and (iii) the simultaneous, intertwined occurrence of horrendous evil and divine hiddenness from devout believers.

Again, we return to this idea that we can perhaps understand relatively minor mishaps and suffering to take place in order to justify a greater good. But persecution and death on industrial scales are much, much harder to justify.

The secret Christian persecution that Nagasawa references (in the work of author Shusaku Endo) details events such as a particularly devout one-eyed man who refused to renounce God and was willing to

---

[1] From Nagasawa's chapter "Silence, evil, and Shusaku Endo" in Green & Stump (2015), p. 249.

die *for God*. And yet, God remained obstinately hidden, causing one to question whether, really, God existed or still exists, or is omnibenevolent.

For Nagasawa, rather like Hopkins, the problem is that highfalutin conceptual ideas about why God might be refusing to act to save people or alleviate their pain does nothing to assuage the sufferers' *experiences*. It is an intellectual solution to an experiential problem, and doesn't do justice to the *actual* suffering. As Nagasawa continues:[1]

> I maintain, however, that theodicies do not eliminate the problem of divine absence altogether because they fail to answer the experiential problem, which concerns the pain and suffering of real people. We are mistaken if we think that theodicies can eliminate the experiential problem; that would perhaps be as absurd as thinking that we could eliminate a toothache with an intellectual argument.

Furthermore, it is not so much about God having a supposed answer or reason or greater good for any suffering, but why God might remain *silent* about it. It is one thing to say that God didn't stop the 2004 tsunami because of some reason X, but that God is not forthcoming about (a) there being a reason at all, and (b) what, exactly, that reason might be (in this case, X). Instead, humans have to pick up the pieces and (a) suppose there *is* a reason *at all*, and (b) work out exactly what that reason might be given that God has decided to remain utterly silent on the matter.

That humans have to guess on behalf of God is part of the problem.

"God moves in mysterious ways," I guess.

But this is not good enough when millions of people have died in a pandemic. This is not good enough when family members are suffering horribly and then dying in front of your very face. Remember, even Abraham had God pretty much appearing and explaining itself to

---

[1] Ibid., p. 254.

him in light of that terrible moral test when his loved one was in the firing line.

The problem with such an experiential argument – for Christians – is that the only way to fully solve the problem is for God to break its silence, and this is something that it routinely and continuously fails to do.

Essentially, the more we find out about the world, the more we are able to measure and record it. The more we understand it, the less we have a need for gods, and the less they apparently interfere in our daily lives and the accounts constructed to explain this world around us.

God has not shaken down city walls, or destroyed armies with supernatural waters, or appeared to masses of people, for a few thousand years. So there are only two rational options:

(a) OmniGod loves playing *really long* games of hide and seek.
(b) OmniGod does not exist.

Now, as much as I love the idea of God still hiding in a cupboard after 2,000 years, I do favour the latter option as being more rational.

Jonathan MS Pearce

Part Five

THE AFTERLIFE

The afterlife developed as an idea partly, I would claim, in light of something called "Just-World Theory". Just-World Theory (or Hypothesis) can also be called the Just-World Fallacy because it is a faulty way of thinking about the world – a sort of cognitive bias.

The idea goes something like this. We have an in-built desire for fairness. We can see this in other primates; there are some fascinating fairness experiments that have been done on bonobos, for example, to show that they have a functional understanding of fairness and justice. However, in having this sense of fairness (which has evolved over time), we accidentally assume that the world – that the universe – is somehow fair.

The problem, as any good skeptic or realist will tell you, is that shit happens. And on some pretty monumental scales. Tsunamis and malaria, famine and drought, genocide and paedophilia – it can be pretty horrible out there.

Our brains invent ways of dealing with the unfairness of an uncaring universe: karma, you reap what you sow, what goes around comes around, he had it coming, and so on.

Unfortunately, when one reaps what one sows, it is either coincidence or other reasons at play. It has nothing to do with a fair universe or God (or gods) seeking to balance the books.

Here is a secular anecdote for you.

When my twin boys were much younger, they were playing on a chair (with wheelie casters) on our tiled kitchen floor, whizzing up and down to much happy laughter. However, we had a large range oven cooker inherited from the previous owners of our then new house. One of the twin four-year-olds (many years later, the precise perpetrator is still open to debate) was responsible for the wheelie chair (with twin rider) flying at top speed into the left-hand oven door.

SMASH.

Door utterly smashed. A couple of seconds of stupidity, and we had a…£1,300 bill! You see, the oven was ten years old and they didn't make the parts for that model, so we had no option but to get a new one.

Thank the cosmos for Google and the ability to search by part number, as I managed to get literally the last oven door I could find from just one spare parts company. So the bill came down to a mere £150…

My partner and I were sitting down talking about this after shouting the boys up to bed. She uttered the words, "The only way I can see it is that it *had* to happen because the oven was faulty and was going to burn the house down anyway…"

She actually gave a couple of reasons why this might have happened. She used to be (socially?) Catholic before we were together. Later, by osmosis due to living with me, she lost her faith. But, despite losing her faith, she is not alone in holding such karmic views about oven doors and other things. Karmic arguments and opinions are extraordinarily commonplace no matter whether you hold faith or not. The idea of this karmic scenario just seems fairer, and we struggle to cope with things not being fair. It's why we like happy endings to films, and just deserts. So when things go wrong, there must be a reason for it.

But for naturalistic atheists, of course, the universe does not work like this. Shit happens. Period. So it is not surprising that an inherent desire for and belief in a just world can lead to (or is a core value in) religiosity and belief. This is especially the case when you believe your god is benevolent and responsible for designing and creating the world.

Thus, if God is fair, then its creation – the universe – must in some sense be fair.

But it is not. It is clearly not.

Going back in time, we can see that the Jews took on the Greek idea of a soul, heaven, and hell precisely on account of bad things happening to good people (the Chosen People, the Jews) under the Hellenistic (Greek-ised) rulers of the Seleucid Empire. How could the Chosen People be so oppressed and disadvantaged?

In this way, we see a gradual development of ideas and understanding of the world until, at this point in time, and in this area of the world, the idea of the afterlife is created in order to serve as the vehicle for karmic fairness.

Quite what heaven and hell are is entirely vague. The Bible, arguably luckily says very little about heaven and hell. There is very little detail indeed. This is lucky because the Bible isn't then nailing incoherent colours to the mast in saying heaven is exactly this, and hell exactly that. If the Bible were that descriptive, philosophers would come along a few hundred years later and point out the outright contradictions and inconsistencies. Perhaps hell is torture and carnage, beasts and boilings. Or perhaps it is eternal inner torment, or isolation from God. For others, it might be the annihilation of the soul – nonexistence. Thus, taking aim at heaven and hell will be difficult because they mean so many different things to different groups of believers.

No one can contest that earthly life seems very unfair to an awful lot of people. A six-month-old baby getting cancer and dying is hard to deal with. Where is that little baby now?

"Well," the naturalist atheist caringly says, "just worm food. Or ashes, depending."

It's not very comforting.

"She's in heaven now, an angel flying amongst family," is a much more comforting idea. The cosmic books are balanced with an eternal afterlife.

And vice versa.

"Hitler killed how many people? And he just shot himself? How is that fair?" asks the shocked just worlder seeking cosmic justice.

"It's not fair when you only think about Earth. It's why he is rotting in hell, being tortured by Satan for eternity," comforts the theist.

So it works both ways: heaven balances the books for those on Earth who have had it tough, and hell balances the books for those on Earth who have made it tough on others.

But in order for heaven and hell to work (and, don't worry, we'll get to those twin destinations in due course), there must first be some vehicle that transcends time and space that can take *us* from *here* to *there*.

The soul...

19 – The Soul Doesn't Exist

Enter stage left…The Soul. It is the greatest *deus ex machina* of all time, getting those who like to create this fair (afterlife) narrative out of a bind. Just by magic, the human being who dies on Earth is somehow transported, meaningfully as *that* human being, to an ethereal location.

Soul this and soul that. The idea of a soul permeates popular culture, from soul music, to feeling things in your soul, to having soul, to having a soulmate, to this and, indeed, that. Souls are a really important part of many theists' theological frameworks.

But what *is* a soul? And what does it *do*?

The answers to these questions are harder to nail down than you might think for something so commonly invoked. Julien Musolino's brilliant chapter "The Soul Fallacy" in John W. Loftus's excellent *Christianity in the Light of Science* elucidates these problematic questions:[1]

> Few ideas have been as widespread and enduring as the belief in the existence and immortality of the human soul. As Mark Baker and Steward Goetz observe in their book The Soul Hypothesis, "Most people, at most times, in most places, at most ages have believed that human beings have some kind of soul." At the dawn of the twenty-first century, soul beliefs still permeate every aspect of our lives. Results from national polls and empirical studies indicate that most Americans, and many more people around the world, believe in the existence and immortality of the soul. Most

---

[1] Musolino in Loftus, John W. (2016), *Christianity in the Light of Science*, Amherst: Prometheus Books, p. 187.

religious doctrines would be unrecognizable if stripped from the claims they make about death and the afterlife. Moreover, these beliefs are constantly reinforced by a wealth of books, articles, TV shows, and pronouncements from writers of all stripes who claim to have found credible scientific evidence for the existence of the soul.

In sharp contrast to popular opinion, most mainstream scientists have abandoned the idea of the soul. This is what Nobel laureate Francis Crick famously called "The Astonishing Hypothesis": "You, your joys and your sorrows, your memories and your ambitions, your sense of personal identity and free will, are in fact no more than the behaviour of a vast assembly of nerve cells and their associated molecules." Echoing Crick's words, Harvard cognitive neuroscientist Joshua Greene explains that while most people are dualists and think of themselves as immaterial minds or souls housed in physical bodies, most psychologists and neuroscientists disagree. The sciences of the mind proceed on the assumption that the mind is simply what the brain does.

The Catholic Encyclopedia attempts to answer these questions with an obviously theistic twist. The opening section here says it all:[1]

The question of the reality of the soul and its distinction from the body is among the most important problems of philosophy, for with it is bound up the doctrine of a future life. Various theories as to the nature of the soul have claimed to be reconcilable with the tenet of immortality, but it is a sure instinct that leads us to suspect every attack on the substantiality or spirituality of the soul as an assault on the belief in existence after death.

---

[1] Maher, M., & Bolland, J. (1912), "Soul", *The Catholic Encyclopedia*, New York: Robert Appleton Company, available online at *New Advent*, https://www.newadvent.org/cathen/14153a.htm (accessed 10/11/2021).

Evidently, we (or, they) are not really sure what it is. However, Christians (in particular) really need the soul as the basis for immortality, and thus for access to heaven and hell. Therefore, the soul is pretty darned important, but also pretty darned mysterious or even incoherent.

St Thomas Aquinas thought as follows, upon which Catholic doctrine is largely built:[1]

- The rational soul, which is one with the sensitive and vegetative principle, is the form of the body. This was defined by the Council of Vienne of 1311.

- The soul is a substance, but an incomplete substance, i.e., it has a natural aptitude and exigency for existence in the body, in conjunction with which it makes up the substantial unity of human nature.

- Though connaturally related to the body, it is itself absolutely simple, i.e., of an unextended and spiritual nature. It is not wholly immersed in matter, its higher operations being intrinsically independent of the organism.

- The rational soul is produced by special creation at the moment when the organism is sufficiently developed to receive it. In the first stage of embryonic development, the vital principle has merely vegetative powers; then a sensitive soul comes into being, educed from the evolving potencies of the organism — later yet, this is replaced by the perfect rational soul, which is essentially immaterial and so postulates a special creative act. Many modern theologians have abandoned this last point of St. Thomas's teaching, and maintain that a fully rational soul is infused into the embryo at the first moment of its existence.

---

[1] Ibid.

The important takeaways here are that the soul is *rational* and that it is *substantially separated from the body*, though related and deriving properties from it. These ideas are not made easy by various authors within the Bible using the term (or a given term to mean the soul) rather ambiguously (at different times meaning the whole body, or person, or spirit, or breath of life).

Philosopher René Descartes famously claimed that the soul was connected to the pineal gland – not something that is held to nowadays.

The *Catholic Encyclopedia* confusingly concludes, however:[1]

> As regards monistic systems generally, it belongs rather to cosmology to discuss them. We take our stand on the consciousness of individual personality, which consciousness is a distinct deliverance of our very highest faculties, growing more and more explicit with the strengthening of our moral and intellectual being. This consciousness is emphatic, as against the figments of a fallaciously abstract reason, in asserting the self-subsistence (and at the same time the finitude) of our being, i.e., it declares that we are *independent* inasmuch as we are truly persons or selves, not mere attributes or adjectives, while at the same time, by exhibiting our manifold limitations, it directs us to a higher Cause on which our being depends.

> Such is the Catholic doctrine on the nature, unity, substantiality, spirituality, and origin of the soul. It is the only system consistent with Christian faith, and, we may add, morals, for both Materialism and Monism logically cut away the foundations of these. The foregoing historical sketch will have served also to show another advantage it possesses – namely, that it is by far the most comprehensive, and at the same time discriminating, synthesis of whatever is best in rival systems. It recognizes the physical conditions of the soul's activity with the Materialist, and its spiritual aspect with the Idealist, while with the Monist it insists on the vital unity of human life. It enshrines the principles of ancient

---

[1] Ibid.

speculation, and is ready to receive and assimilate the fruits of modern research.

This is wholly unsatisfying. Indeed, reading the entry, one comes away thinking it is just a ruse to confuse the reader so much that they forget why they were coming to read the piece in the first place. There is no real, easily discernible definition of what a soul is or does, merely lots of discussion of the idea over history.

Perhaps Christian philosopher Richard Swinburne can help (from *The Evolution of the Soul*):[1]

> It is a frequent criticism of substance dualism[2] that dualists cannot say what souls are. Souls are immaterial subjects of mental properties. They have sensations and thoughts, desires and beliefs, and perform intentional actions. Souls are essential parts of human beings.

But here we have the soul doing exactly what the physical body and emergent mind already do. Swinburne essentially says the soul is immaterial, psychologically potent in some way, and immortal.

The problem with any claims about the soul is that they end up being theological assertions with no evidence to back them up. Because, if we could *provide evidence of* what souls were, we would *know* what souls were. It is pretty obvious. If souls had tangible effects on this world, on us, we would be able to measure them in some way. So a soul ends up becoming something that is unevidenced, and this is why there is disagreement (amongst Christians, for example) over what it really is.

Here are some of the problems for soul proponents:

---

[1] Swinburne, Richard (1997), *The Evolution of the Soul*, Oxford: Oxford University Press, p. 333.
[2] The belief that mind and body are two different things or entities, having two completely different substances, and opposed to the mind identifying physically with the brain.

- The soul needs to be meaningfully connected to the earthly agent so that you can identify the soul in heaven or hell as of the same person on Earth.

- This must include moral culpability. If the soul is being punished or rewarded, it must have some kind of culpability for that which it is being punished or rewarded. Thus, it must somehow be causally involved in decisions or actions on Earth that are being judged.

- It cannot be explained by things that are already explicable in human science. Therefore, rationality, memory, personality and anything understood by neurology, consciousness, genetics and other scientific areas cannot be the purview of the soul.

- The only escape from (3) seems to be that anything not yet understood about consciousness is plugged by "the soul". This is the "soul of the gaps" argument, as I like to label it.

There are other issues I could add here but which I am saving for later arguments.

If souls are to be rational, what really differentiates them from consciousness? Though we don't fully understand consciousness, we know it supervenes[1] on the brain. Without the brain, we are not conscious. Moreover, if you take drugs, are tired or hungry, or stick a fork into your eye socket and into your brain, your consciousness *will* be affected (don't try this last one at home, please). These are all physical and easily evidenced things. The physical world defines the mental world. I refer you back to Musolino's previously mentioned chapter "The Soul Fallacy" for the whole suite of arguments against the soul existing.

In order to be rational, and yet be separate from the brain and consciousness, I am not sure what the soul can be. If

---

[1] Depends on or emerges from.

it *is* consciousness, then it is...consciousness, and it will die with your brain.

If it is rational and separate from your consciousness, then what part does it play in your life throughout your living years? What does it *actually do* that your consciousness does not? If we are judged either at death or contemporaneously for the decisions our conscious brains make, then what is the soul in this context? What responsibility or part in those actions does it have or play? Is it just a carbon copy or reflection of the consciousness that can continue after brain death? If so, it would have to be invisibly connected to the body in some mysterious way. And if this were the case, then it would play no causal role in your actual life, being merely a photocopy of that which does.

We understand the parts of the brain involved in rational processes. And so making the same claims about the soul is to special plead this can happen *without the physical matter of the brain*.

If the soul is rational, but *not* connected to or reflective of lived consciousness, then in what state is the soul representing me in heaven? How is it rational such that it is in any way reflective of my everyday conscious rationality but not *actually* my everyday rationality? This is a veritable two-horned dilemma.

The other end of the human timeline is equally fraught with problems. When do humans become ensouled? If it is at conception, then there are some pretty big hurdles for the soul thesis. For example, certain twin embryos don't develop until some amount of time after conception, so this model can't work, or must be radically altered ad hoc. Another hurdle is IVF (in vitro fertilisation). Fertilised embryos, arguably ensouled with supposedly rational properties and identity, are frozen, in theory *indefinitely*. What happens to this rational entity as the embryo – that early human physical form – is frozen indefinitely? Is there some soul bar in the netherworld where they hang out until they are summoned back?

It's interesting to wonder how a one-day-old embryo can have any rational properties (or the soul). If the soul has rational properties at this stage, then that rationalism has nothing to do with the developed rationalism (dependent on the brain and life of the later individual) that is created over time by that which eventually becomes a person. We understand how and why rationality develops through infancy and up into adulthood, and how it can decline in old age. And the soul is not part of the explanatory framework.

The soul cannot account for this and, in fact, becomes even more incoherent.

Personally, I am not at all sold on the idea of a soul.

20 – What's the Point of (Heaven and) Hell?

As mentioned earlier, the idea that we don't have libertarian free will is also terminal for belief in heaven and hell. That most philosophers now deny libertarian free will is interesting for two reasons:

(1) It turns out almost all the philosophers who *do* believe in libertarian free will (about 13.7%)[1] also believe in God. Thus, it looks like they believe in libertarian free will not because it is rational, but because they need it to make sense of the god they believe in.

(2) The free will argument seems somewhat old hat now. What most secular philosophers are more interested in is what we do with this knowledge. Much more time and energy is spent working out the ramifications on moral responsibility, crime and punishment.

On this later point, it is worth noting that prison is understood to fulfil three functions: *retribution*, *deterrence*, and *rehabilitation*. As we understand more and more about the causality of human behaviour and crime, we find retribution less and less important. It is somewhat

---

[1] The biggest ever survey of philosophers, the *PhilPapers* Survey: "The PhilPapers Surveys", *PhilPapers*, https://philpapers.org/surveys/results.pl (accessed 10/11/2021). The metadata analysis of this question shows the overwhelming correlation between those who argue for libertarian free will and those who believe in God, and it is certainly the case that a judgemental god requires this notion of free will to hold. Thus, the correlation seems to be underwritten by this causation.

rationally unwarranted, if still a natural reaction. Modern prisons in the countries with the lowest recidivism rates (the rate of *re*offending) concentrate more on rehabilitation than on the other two.

In the US, it doesn't look good for recidivism:[1]

> Two reports on long-term recidivism among prisoners released from state and federal prisons showed very high arrest rates. The rate for state prisoners was 83% over a nine-year study period, while it was 39.8% for nonviolent and about 64% for violent federal prisoners over an eight-year period.
>
> A May 2018 U.S. Department of Justice report on state prisoner recidivism followed a sample of the 412,731 prisoners released by 30 states in 2005 - about 77% of all state prisoners released that year. Of those releasees, 89% were male, 18% were under age 24 and 54% were between 25 and 39. Blacks and whites each made up about 40% of the releasees. Of the entire study group, 32% had been convicted of drug offenses, 30% of property offenses, 26% of violent crimes and 13% of public order offenses.
>
> Overall, almost 45% of the former prisoners were arrested within one year of release; 16% were arrested for the first time in the second year, 8% in the third, 11% in years four to six and 4% in years seven to nine. Thus, about 68% were arrested within three years, 79% within six years and 83% in nine years.

Norway, on the contrary, has prisons that are often accused by old-school punitive thinkers as being soft-touch. But they end up being the most successful – these low recidivism rates (about 20%) are more effective with taxpayers' money as the prisons are not treated as

---

[1] Clarke, Matthew (2019), "Long-Term Recidivism Studies Show High Arrest Rates", *Prison Legal News*, https://www.prisonlegalnews.org/news/2019/may/3/long-term-recidivism-studies-show-high-arrest-rates/ (accessed 01/11/2021).

revolving doors accepting the same criminals year after year. Norway has even banned life sentences.[1]

The outlook for a prison system is transformative: these are human beings whose causal circumstances have led to criminality, but who, in many cases, are able to be turned around – transformed – and reintroduced to society to become fully functioning and integrated members. There is a strong sense of linking policies on crime and punishment with those of fighting poverty.

In other words, without our divine foreknowledge, we are arguably starting to do a better job of effective punishment of crime than OmniGod with all its knowledge, and its outdated understanding of retributive punishment in hell with no hope of transformation and redemption forever.

Deterrence is also an interesting idea. Theists might claim that threatening people with hell is a great deterrence. After all, there is no worse punishment.

However, it turns out that harsher punishments do not lead to more effective deterrence. This is something of a myth (and one, I should think, OmniGod would be aware of…). Harsher punishment has a negligible effect on whether one will commit a crime or not. On the other hand, certainty of being caught is a far greater deterrent.

And yet, even though OmniGod should make all people certain of being caught, it is only really earthly certainty that works.

In fact, the US Department of Justice's National Institute of Justice is very clear on deterrence, in summing up the research:[2]

- The certainty of being caught is a vastly more powerful deterrent than the punishment.
- Sending an individual convicted of a crime to prison isn't a very effective way to deter crime.

[1] "Norway's Prison System Benefits Its Economy", *The Borgen Project*, (2020), https://borgenproject.org/norways-prison-system/ (accessed 01/11/2021).
[2] "Five Things about Deterrence", *National Institute of Justice*, (2016) https://www.ojp.gov/pdffiles1/nij/247350.pdf (accessed 01/11/2021).

- Police deter crime by increasing the perception that criminals will be caught and punished.
- Increasing the severity of punishment does little to deter crime.
- There is no conclusive evidence that the death penalty deters criminals.

We need to throw away old-fashioned ideas about crime and punishment if we are going to deal as effectively and humanely as we can with it.

Which is to say, rather clearly and loudly, that hell is neither effective nor humane. It does not transform people because it appears (there is very little data on hell, even from holy books like the Bible – it's generally a case of making stuff up) that those condemned to hell stay in hell. End of story.

The point of hell, therefore, is not to rehabilitate. And yet to rehabilitate is what we do with criminals when we want to be the most humane, the most compassionate, the most...*loving*, and to run the most socially cohesive society. Instead, hell is more about retribution and deterrence.

But here's the further problem. Who is the retribution for? We humans have no idea who the heck goes to hell and who doesn't. We might *think* we do, but we don't actually know. We don't know whether, just before he pulled the trigger, Hitler asked for redemption and accepted Jesus into his life. So retribution is only for God himself.

Let's get this right. God designs and creates the universe knowing the outcome before creating. God creates a group of entities with the full knowledge (before creating them) that they will go to hell, and creates them anyway. And then it sends them to hell for eternity out of some sense of indignation and retribution?

"Ha! That'll teach you (for me designing you like that knowing you would do that)! I'm going to punish you FOREVER! Ah ha ha!"

Or, and this is just an idea, maybe God shouldn't create those people in the first place...

There isn't too much solid data out there, but one interesting piece of research found that belief in hell *did lower* crime rates, whilst belief in heaven *increased* crime rates![1]

> The present analysis has uncovered two strong, unique, and reliable relations between religious belief and national crime rates. The degree to which a country's rate of belief in heaven outstrips its rate of belief in hell significantly predicts higher national crime rates. Statistically, this finding manifests in two independent effects: the strong negative effect of rates of belief in hell on crime, and the strong positive effect of rates of belief in heaven on crime. Both of these effects follow from predictions based on recent laboratory findings and on theories that ascribe socio-cultural functions of religions. Indeed, these findings coalesce with theoretical and empirical work suggesting that beliefs in punishing and omniscient supernatural agents spread across historical societies primarily because of their ability to foster cooperation and suppress anti-social behavior among anonymous strangers.

Whilst there may be *some* deterrent value entailed with the idea of hell, this appears negated by the belief in heaven. Also, it is hard to make sense of such deterrence when no one is quite sure whether hell really happens, what it is like, and how long it really goes on for. The retributive element certainly makes no sense. And the rehabilitative element is non-existent.

All in all, hell makes no sense. And, if the claims of many theists are to be believed, it appears to be a pretty despicable place that only provides *God* with anything "useful" or "meaningful" at all – a cosy sense of retribution, which is in turn invalidated by its own foreknowledge of who goes to hell anyway. All hell really offers for

---

[1] Sharriff, Azim & Rhemtulla, Mijke (2012), "Divergent Effects of Beliefs in Heaven and Hell on National Crime Rates", *PLoS One*, https://www.ncbi.nlm.nih.gov/pmc/articles/PMC3377603/ (accessed 01/11/2021).

humans is an eternity of torture for finite crimes that God knew would happen, and created humans anyway in such a way *that it would happen*, knowing that some of these entities would be condemned for evermore.

Lovely.

21 – God Cannot Be Perfectly Merciful and Perfectly Just

This argument is well-trodden; I'm just not so sure that the theistic answers cut the mustard.

First, let's unpack the terms. First, *just*. I would define this to mean "acting or being in conformity with what is merited or deserved". On the other hand, *merciful* means, "acting with forbearance shown especially to an offender or to someone subject to one's power; acting leniently or compassionately".

The problem is, there is some degree of mutual exclusivity with these terms. However, these are both terms that supposedly apply to God. Perfect justice demands that someone receives the full punishment that they merit (leaving no room for a reduction in punishment), and yet to be perfectly merciful is to forgive when there is the ability to fully punish. As the great preacher turned atheist Dan Barker says of this in his book *Godless*:[1]

> During the debate, Rajabali said that Allah is a "just" God, as well as an "infinitely merciful" God, so I jumped at the rare opportunity to positively disprove the existence of God, as so defined. Justice means that punishment is administered with the exact amount of severity that is deserved for the crime that is committed. We don't put children in prison for stealing cookies, and we don't merely fine a murderer $50. Mercy, on the other hand, means that punishment is

---

[1] Barker, Dan (2008), *Godless*, Berkeley, CA: Ulysses Press, p. 79-80.

administered with less severity than deserved. When the police officer lets you off with a warning instead of a ticket for breaking the speed limit, that is mercy.

If God is infinitely merciful, he can never be just. If God is ever just (not to mention infinitely just), then he cannot be infinitely merciful. A God who is both infinitely merciful and just not only does not exist, he cannot exist. This is one of the positive arguments for the nonexistence of God based on incompatible properties (or incoherency). If God is defined as a married bachelor, we don't need to discuss evidence or argument; we can simply claim a logical impossibility. In response, Rajabali chided me for failing to think in multiple dimensions at the same time. "When Qur'an says God is Merciful, and God is Just," he went on, "these simultaneous characteristics cannot be compartmentalized, we must understand them holistically." I guess that explains it.

By the way, I also pointed out that if God is infinitely merciful, then I cannot go to hell. It wouldn't matter how I lived or what I thought, infinite mercy would absolve me of any crime, no matter how great, including the crime of refusing to believe in God, accept his authority or admit that I had done anything wrong.

Theistic manoeuvres often attempt to either redefine the words enough for them to work together, or, in a Christian context, claim that Jesus' sacrifice makes up for the justice part.

Except, with all the pain and suffering in the world – from genocide to malaria, cancer to plate tectonics – God appears not to be at all merciful. And when it comes to eternal damnation in hell, God is clearly not being perfectly merciful. Everywhere we look, notwithstanding the contradiction, there is *prima facie*[1] evidence that God is *not* perfectly merciful.

---

[1] Face-value or obvious evidence.

So when we are told that God is simultaneously perfectly just and perfectly merciful, we are right to stop and question this assertion. Because it makes no sense.

22 – Weighing Our Hearts: Heaven or Hell?

How much do our hearts weigh? This depends on how they are weighed and what the metrics are. Stay with me here.

There is a debate that has long been raging in Christianity, for example, as to whether the defining criteria for entering heaven is *faith* or *belief* in God or Jesus as opposed to *good works* or *deeds*. This is relevant to the previous argument about the accidents of geography and history and how unfair it is if God has arranged the world in such a way. The problem is twofold:

(1) If faith alone gets us into heaven, then most people throughout history and geography have been, are, and will be unable to access the right belief or faith. Therefore, God is unfair in condemning those people to hell (or not heaven).

(2) If it is works or deeds (being a good person) that get us into heaven, then we don't need to believe in any given God, or certainly not, say, Jesus. This somewhat calls into question the point of the belief system and the churches of the world.

Perhaps there is a third option – in that it is a combination of the two. Of course, there have been many in-depth theological wrangles employing vast arrays of biblical texts to try and work this out, with Christian thinkers sitting on all sides.

Either way, there are further problems to compound the philosophical misery of those who ascribe to the problematic notions of heaven and hell.

Imagine a good person who is faithful and acts incredibly morally for eighty years of their life, but becomes a mass-murdering maniac for the last week. A really terrible human being at the end of their life. Then imagine the opposite: a really terrible, Hitleresque human for eighty years who then repents to be lovely and faithful for their last week on Earth.

Who gets to heaven? Why? How is this calculated?

Here is an *actual quote* from a US pastor representing an *actual theological belief*. This is Pastor Michael Cesar speaking to his congregation:[1]

> "Not that I would ever do this, but if you gave me an AK-47 right now with enough ammo to take you all out and, before I did it, I started blaspheming the Holy Ghost's name and then took you out and then put the gun in my mouth...I *still* end up in heaven. Sorry. That probably wouldn't happen as before I got to do it, the Lord would stop me. He might take me out before I got my finger on the trigger! But that's the power of the salvation...it's all the work of the Lord."

This sort of incredible claim is actually fairly commonplace, and it's pretty incredible. Because this pastor has been "saved", he can apparently do anything and walk through the pearly gates.

This makes no moral sense whatsoever.

Let's continue thinking about the range of moral behaviours and beliefs.

What about someone who is 49.9% good (whether through faith or deeds or both) – not quite reaching the 50% threshold (or whatever the threshold might be)? Are they to be equally condemned as the 1%

[1] 'Matthew 7:12-29 "The Broad Way and the Narrow"', *Pastor Michael Cesar M D*, https://www.youtube.com/watch?v=Tn4-4sJFFks (accessed 28/10/2021).

person? Likewise, is the 50.1% person entitled to the same paradise as the 99% person?

The only way around this, it seems to me, is to do away with heaven and hell and have a single sliding scale afterlife that directly reflects whatever outcome calculation God weighs up for each individual's earthly life.

Despite being intuitively attractive, this sliding scale does not seem evidenced or claimed in major holy books. It also looks like moulding an idea as a post hoc rationalisation to fit a preconceived assertion that heaven and hell, in some way, must exist.

Do babies go to heaven? Do they get there as babies? Are they measured on what they would have done had they grown to be adults? Then, if God can imagine all counterfactuals, perhaps someone who goes to hell in world W1 would actually have had a life that would have got them to heaven in W2. So it's unfair for this person to be created in a world that condemns them to hell when God could have created them in a world that got them to heaven.

This makes for some fascinating thought experiments. Is it the case that an agent (Anja) goes to hell in W1, but to get around the aforementioned problem, would go to hell in *all* possible worlds? This would mean God would be creating a contingent (one that need not exist but does as a result of God's creative nature) entity that *necessarily* has a certain outcome when created. This is incredibly unfair for Anja, who has no control at all over whether she gets created. She is destined to fail in every possible world in which she is created.

The other side of the coin, as mentioned, is that there are some worlds that God could create, but doesn't, where Anja ends up going to heaven. But God doesn't create those worlds, just W1 (because God cannot create multiple worlds of different counterfactuals but with the *same* souls, since you would get souls going to both heaven and hell at the same time!). So, without any choice in the matter, Anja is back to being committed to hell in W1 – a world that God decided to design and create – when she *could* have gone to heaven in W2. God has condemned Anja without Anja being able to do the slightest thing about it.

Heaven and hell do not make any sense. OmniGod does not make any sense.

Alas, there is more.

23 – Explaining the Heaven Me

It's not just *how* we get to heaven, but what we *look like* when we get there. A real problem for the soul is the very thing it is supposed to function for: carrying on after death. When we die, it is generally assumed by theists that the soul is the immortal entity that continues our existence into whatever realm we are deemed justified in inhabiting.[1] If we go to heaven, however, if the soul looks like consciousness, then what part of our life is the soul supposed to represent?

We've discussed this a little, but let's go further in looking at how the idea works in the contexts of heaven and hell.

Imagine I am an eighty-year-old person who has severe dementia and I go to heaven. Do I take that dementia with me as that was "me" at death? I have lost most aspects of my former personality, the one that my family and friends know me by, and my faculties have all but disappeared. Surely, this is me for heaven, right? Wandering around, lost, barely remembering who I am, and not remembering the people I miss, living in a sad confusion.

Or do we get some kind of cherry-picking of representation throughout my life? Is it "me" five years before death, ten, twenty? If not, at what point? How is this decided? If the soul is a photocopy, when is that photocopy made?

Or is it an amalgam, an average of properties that you have throughout life? In this way, the version of us in heaven is actually not a

---

[1] Unless the theist is an annihilationist that believes that the soul is destroyed at death.

version of you that ever *really* existed, but an averaged-out you, thus making the representation of you in heaven somewhat disconnected to who you were on Earth.

What about any number of shortcomings that I may have with my personality? There may be things that are incongruous with a life in heaven. I may be a little quick to anger, or somewhat jealous in certain situations, but not enough to invalidate my entrance to heaven. You can think of all sorts of scenarios like this – I'm a good person but I like to occasionally take Class A drugs. Or I'm a decent person but I have this or that vice. Do these personality traits and vices get eradicated so that I am being fundamentally *changed* for access through the pearly gates, so that I am not at odds with the idea of heaven?

What about if a baby or a foetus dies? Are they just sitting in heaven as a baby, unable to do anything but blissfully sit there smiling (but certainly not crying!)? What about a blastocyst? Are they sitting in heaven as clusters of cells without any kind of consciousness, ability to experience, or rationality?

Or are souls a *potential* you? Who you could become in some utopia? But there are just as many issues with this as any other supposed solutions, as we saw at the end of the last chapter, where we discussed which potential world God might choose to put us in.

We can try to get around this problem. But not successfully. We return to our previous issues, such that if my soul is merely tenuously "connected" to my conscious self (and thus all my memories and sense of self), then it ends up being essentially unrelated to "me" – the entity being judged in the first place. It's like a balloon I am holding, but that plays no active part in who I am and the decisions I make; it just floats alongside, tethered by a fragile thread.

The other option is to bend the idea of heaven so much that it can somehow accommodate all of the many criticisms that can be levelled against it. We *could* do this, I suppose, because the revelatory guidance for heaven is so nebulous that people can make of it what they want. I'm just not sure that, even starting from philosophical scratch, you can make ideas of heaven and hell work, especially when confusing them with broken ideas like libertarian free will and souls.

24 – Free Will, the Problem of Evil, and Heaven

I clearly can't get enough of free will arguments. Or those concerning the afterlife. This is a match made in heaven…

Before we get onto talking about heaven, let's unpack earthly free will a little bit more.

The Free Will Theodicy is one of the get-out-of-jail free cards used by many apologists to at least partly rebut the problem of evil. Why is there so much suffering in the world given an OmniGod? The theodicy states that the corollary of giving humans the wonderful gift of free will is that they will, necessarily so (given human nature), make bad decisions. They will choose badly, and this results in pain and suffering. And suffering is a necessary by-product of the good of free will.

But is this the case?

Well, there are two points to make in reply to this claim.

1. Heaven

If heaven exists, then (it is normally argued) there is no pain of suffering therein. And yet, (it is also argued), on Earth, humans *must* live with the suffering that comes as collateral from the usage of free will. In theory, free will is a really good thing. But if there is no free will in heaven (since there can be no suffering), and heaven is supposed to be the place where humans exist in some kind of perfection, then free will *can't* be "all that and a bag of chips". For free will to be used as a consequentialist theodicy, the overriding benefit of free will outweighs the evil and suffering that comes with it (i.e., the bad choices resultant from the free will).

If free will is *such* a beneficial and great-making thing, then surely it *must* exist in heaven, or we merely become heavenly automata – precisely what theists argue against. Of course, we have seen it argued that God must have it, too. But if God has free will, and it is perfect, it can only choose the most perfect, most loving thing; and so, as we have seen, God cannot have free will either!

Essentially, heaven must exist with both free will *and* a lack of suffering and evil. If it can be done up there, why not down here?

Furthermore, as I point out in the next chapter, it is surely remiss of God not, then, to create *only* heaven. God should create only those whom it knows (in advance since it knows all the counterfactuals) will freely come to love him, and create Earth as it is in heaven, to quote, you know, a prayer about his will that is recited almost every Sunday in a Christian church near you.

Which leads me onto:

2. Logical Necessity

The Free Will Theodicy seems to suggest that free will *logically necessitates* evil decisions being made. But this does not appear to be the case. It is not *logically necessary* that humans will choose badly every single time, though it might be very *probable indeed* that they do. But you could envisage a group of people who could *possibly* choose benignly every single time. This is a conceptual or logical *possibility*.

The flipside would be that choosing morally positively *every time* is a logical *impossibility*, not just an inductive probability. What kind of creation is that whereby God has designed us to fail or cause suffering no matter what? There seems to be a two-horned dilemma here for the believer. Either we are designed and created such that it is logically impossible for us to choose well every time (causing suffering), or God has chosen those of us when creating who would just happen to choose badly (also causing suffering). Thus, God chooses to select people who will cause pain and suffering due to their own free will, and stopping it would perhaps go against its own free will.

The main point is that there is nothing logically standing in the way of benign human behaviour (though it may be unlikely). God *could* create a set of humans who (given the existence of libertarian free will, which I contest) would just so happen to choose correctly every single time, thus minimising evil and suffering that might come about from poor freely willed choices.

So there are two issues here. First, it is not necessary that free will causes pain and suffering, only probable. And thus God does not *have* to create a world in which suffering *does* take place as a result of human free will. Second, this is either evidenced in heaven – free will *does* exist (because it must do so unless we are to be robotic automata in heaven) and yet there is no suffering. Or free will does not exist in heaven, in which case we are just heavenly automata. The latter option renders heaven somewhat incoherent and is a good argument that it does not exist. Either way, you get problems on Earth or problems in heaven as a result of how theists like to argue about free will.

Here endeth the lesson.

25 – Why Not Just Create Heaven?

As if there weren't enough problems already, let's make life even more difficult for the proponent of OmniGod. This one is simple: Why not just create us in heaven?

If the endgame is eternal existence in the afterlife – one or the other of the final destinations – then we can arguably advocate for skipping to the end straight away. This isn't like simply forward winding a film until you get to the end. In that scenario, people can complain that you are missing out on the joy of the film. In the movie of life, unlike a Hollywood movie, you get starvation, plagues, tsunamis, genocides, and countless other ways of suffering and dying horribly.

Skipping to the end, in this scenario, sounds quite reasonable. Or morally required. Especially if you know the journey – the journey of suffering for all those unfortunate ones.

Moreover, an omniscient god with full divine foreknowledge would also know each and every entity – soul, person, human, whatever – that will go to heaven or will go to hell. Indeed, it appears to create entities *so that* they go to heaven and *so that* they go to hell. This is morally dubious, because God is creating entities in order that they all suffer on Earth, and in order that they suffer eternally in an afterlife.

This is morally repugnant when the alternative is to simply create all the people God would know would "freely come to love it" in heaven. This would eliminate (or not create, rather) the material reality of Earth with all of its suffering. God would also not create all of the entities that it would know in advance would go to hell.

This scenario evades several things:

(1) Any suffering at all on Earth.

(2) Any interminable suffering at all for eternity in hell.

And doesn't that sound morally better? Doesn't that sound compassionate? Doesn't that sound like the sort of thing an *all*-loving god would do?

This was brought up in debate by philosopher Ray Bradley and Christian apologist William Lane Craig some years ago. Bradley formulated the argument slightly differently, as follows. Imagine God knew in advance that 10% of people would freely come to love it in this world. Let's call this world W1. 10% of all people created freely come to love God in W1. So, why doesn't God create only those people in W1? Well, Craig claimed that in creating only those 10% in this alternative world (let's call it W2), this new scenario of fewer people interacting and living would change the dynamics and scenario. Instead of the outcome of these people freely coming to love God as they did in W1, in W2, perhaps only 84% of this new set (the 10% subset who freely came to love God in W1) would now love God in this new scenario W2. So it is infeasible here that God could just create the original subset of people who would come to love it in W1 on their own, because not all of them would now come to love God with this change in scenario and dynamics.

Craig attempts to extricate himself from this tough bind by using the term *unfeasible*. He says, among other things:[1]

> "Some people might be damned if created in some circumstances but saved if they were created in other circumstances. So you can't just divide the line down the middle and put people on either half if it depends upon what world these possible persons are put into."

---

[1] "The Problem of Hell: Raymond Bradley vs. William Lane Craig (Debate)", *Tactopta Chess*, https://www.youtube.com/watch?v=oJdlO6esWr8 (accessed 28/10/2021).

Craig says perhaps there is no *feasible* world that God could create where *everybody* is saved by freely coming to love it. This looks rather like God is not omnipotent and/or not omniscient – that it doesn't have the ability or nous to create such a world of freely loving individuals. Craig uses *feasible* as a term to wriggle out of the problem, as if God is somehow victim to the vagaries of different scenarios in this particular domain. But this is *not* logically impossible…for God.

In this debate, Craig was actually bettered by Bradley at this point. He had no answer, and the audience were left with a bit of silence. A rare thing. But I don't think Bradley needed to talk about the creation of different worlds at all. God merely needed to *imagine* W1, recognise who would come to freely love it, and *then* create those people not in W1 or W2 or W3, but directly in heaven.

Any other worldly creation is a knowing creation and consequent condemnation of hosts of people and animals (and perhaps aliens) to suffering and damnation.

The only way to get God out of jail here is to posit some appeal to skeptical theism – we don't know the mind of God and it moves in mysterious ways. One of these mysteries is that, somehow, there is a greater good that comes out of people and animals existing in material reality that trumps the entirety of suffering and death and pain across the whole universe throughout the sum totality of temporal existence.

This is quite some appeal to quite an unknown. But it's all the theist has and it – for me – falls well short of being persuasive.

God should have known its chosen ones and created them in heaven. No hell, no pain, no suffering, no knowing condemnation to earthly or underworldly suffering.

Easy.

For God.

Right?

26 – Satan Is God's Middle Manager

God is supposed to be omnipotent, all-powerful, almighty. The great-making characteristics of such a god are the paragon of abilities. It could achieve *anything* at the metaphorical click of its fingers. The "fact" that Satan still exists should tell you all you need to know about this problem.

So what the hell is Satan still doing hanging around? Well, of course, Satan doesn't exist either. But suppose you believe that both God and Satan are real entities. Well, then, you'd be making no sense at all. In the UK, there is a flagship interfaith dialogue show called *The Big Questions* on the BBC (a show I was once featured on). I remember some years back on it they were discussing whether the Devil was real, symbolic, or non-existent. A good proportion of the audience advanced different theories on Satan's ontological reality. This annoyed me. None of the speakers and thinkers, movers and shakers, were able to recognise the glaring issue with OmniGod and Satan coexisting as if in some eternal battle of good versus evil.

The philosophical "reality" is that OmniGod could make Satan disappear, non-existent, at the click of its fingers. Any ontological argument for God, or claim that it is perfect, such as under Perfect Being Theology, argues for God's supreme omni-abilities. This has been discussed here at length. God is supposedly the greatest being in conception. Hence, there can be no rival being to God, since God could dispense with any rival on a whim.

This means that if the Devil exists, he[1] does so on the behest of God. Either God *actively* wants him to exist such that his disappearance would cause more grief than good, like some embodiment of the problem of evil. Or God *omits* doing anything about his existence as some kind of *passive* will.

The upshot is that it appears that Satan, if he exists, is doing a job for God; he is providing a service, if you will. Where God is the CEO, Satan is a management executive for God. Therefore, God must accept corporate responsibility for him. In other words, anything that is laid at the invisible feet of Satan, in terms of blame and moral responsibility, should actually be laid at the invisible feet of God. God allows or even plans (either by design, direct causation, or act of omission) everything that Satan does.

These two types of will (active and omissive or permissive) are essentially the same – functionally and meaningfully. If God simply allows something to come to pass without doing anything about it, then God is actively being passive! But if God also has full divine foreknowledge and was to know about all future events including its own actions, then it would have known before creation what Satan would do and still *actively* chose to actualise this particular world. To explain the difference between omissive/permissive will and active will, let us return to the example of the 2004 tsunami. It can be seen in two ways:

(1) God *actively* wanted the tsunami to happen, killing 230,000 people (for some reason), and purposefully caused it to take place. OmniGod brought it about.

(2) God *omitted* doing anything to stop it. Perhaps it was as a result of the way it designed plate tectonics. But when the tsunami came along, even though God was perfectly able to, the supreme being did nothing to prevent it. Remember, though, that God designed and created the world knowing that this would happen.

---

[1] Not sure about the sex or gender of Satan. I'll have to think on it...

Both options are functionally the same. God had the power to stop it, or not to cause it in the first place, but didn't. There must have been greater reasons for the tsunami to take place than for it not to. We are still waiting on those. This is of course made worse for God's culpability when it designed the world in such a way that it happened, and God knew it would.

Now let us apply this kind of logic to Satan. The two options look like this:

(1) God *actively* wants Satan to exist and to do what Satan does – cause havoc and be evil. Thus, Satan is God's underling by active will, doing its bidding like some evil henchman.

(2) God *allows* Satan to do what Satan wants. God has the power to stop Satan at any point, but chooses not to. Satan does what God wants by God omitting to do anything about Satan's actions. Indeed, Satan is not *destroyed* by God.

According to certain fundamentalist, evangelical, and literalist believers, Satan still exists and still does evil. This either admits God's lack of power in not being able to control or destroy the devil, or admits that Satan is providing a service that God wants or needs.

I see no way out of the dilemma here for the Satan-believing theist. Essentially, everything that the devil does is what God wants to happen.

Otherwise, it wouldn't happen. Because God is omnipotent.

Taking this one step further, if the theist believes in Satan doing satanic things, then this must be the case within the paradigm of OmniGod. Satan plants fossils to fool evolutionists, or Satan causes the mass murderer to decide to murder, or Satan does this or that. It is all part of God being omnibenevolent.

Satan's existence provides a greater good.

Necessarily.

There can be no *gratuitous* pain or suffering in God's creations, otherwise this would invalidate God's label of being all-loving.

Therefore, Satan's existence is necessary for, or certainly still allows for, God to be labelled all-loving.

Which renders the whole scenario rather silly and nonsensical – any amount of evil appears to (luckily) be explicable, as we saw in the problem of evil section.

As a reminder, we could also take on here Stephen Maitzen's earlier argument about moral paralysis for the theist. It appears that the theist should do nothing to stop Satan doing his bidding because this would stop the greater good that would necessarily come about from the satanic evil!

27 – Infinite Punishment for Finite Crimes

Crimes are finite. They last a finite amount of time and their effects are not eternal.

On the other hand, heaven and hell are eternal rewards and punishments for getting it right or wrong in our brief time here on Earth.

We don't need to get into the nitty-gritty of what influences human behaviour (you escaped having to read 200 pages on that for the free will argument – just). But humans are at a minimum heavily influenced or determined by the nine elements I previously listed, amongst the myriad causal variables that might be at play:

(1) Being born.
(2) Their genetic inheritance.
(3) Their life in the womb, shaping their genetic self.
(4) Their time and place of birth.
(5) Their parents, relatives, race and gender; their nurture and experiences in infancy and childhood.
(6) The mutations in their brain and body throughout life; and other purely random events.
(7) Their natural physical stature, looks, smile and voice; intelligence; sexual drive and proclivities; personality and wit; and natural ability in sports, music and dance.
(8) Their religious training; economic circumstances; cultural influences; political and civil rights; the prevailing customs of their times.

(9) The blizzard of experiences throughout life, not chosen by them but which happened to them. All the molecules, particles, forces and wave functions; i.e. the environment.

We can so often understand atypical or problematic behaviour, and if we don't, we certainly *seek* to. We (as police, psychologists, society) don't throw our hands up in the air and say, "Ah, it was just free will", and then close the case file and send the miscreant away for eternity.

But that's what happens when people are sent to heaven or hell. And remember that such people and destinations were themselves known and predicted, and therefore designed to be that way, *before* creation.

The only vaguely reasonable attempts to answer why an infinite punishment is appropriate for a finite crime are as follows:

(1) The finite crime is a sin against an infinite being,
(2) You continue to sin in hell.

The first answer sounds nice but I'm not sure it really makes any sense to me. And it makes no more sense if reversed and applied to good deeds and heaven. Do finite good deeds really deserve infinite reward? A further problem in the eternal nature of reward/punishment is that it fails to account for the differences in misdemeanours. Genocidal Hitler infinitely sins against God, and receives eternal punishment, as does someone stealing a loaf of bread (or any level of wrongdoing in between). In fact, since all humans are sinners in one way or another, all humans have infinitely sinned against God, from Mother Theresa to Adolf Hitler.

It's yet another big hot philosophical mess.

The second answer, one that I have seen a few times, is merely an assertion someone makes about hell whilst knowing nothing about it. Sort of a desperate attempt to justify eternal punishment. But if you knew continuing to sin would keep you in hell, in endless torment, why would you keep sinning?

The reality is that many people have a very simplistic understanding of hell that fits in line with their intuitive and emotive psyche. This is nicely summarised in an online comment answering the question "Is there a way to reconcile all of these issues with the unfairness of hell?":[1]

> The short answer is "Yes." Where I grew up, Hell was a very real place, and I knew that many people would end up there. It was reconciled a few ways:
>
> (1) "They deserve it." If you take on an "us vs. them" mindset, and view other people as bad, you don't worry so much about them going to hell.
>
> (2) "Everybody can make a choice - God reveals Himself to all." Everybody who is going to Hell is going there because of their choice. So it's their fault.
>
> (3) "Don't talk about it." That became the most common way to reconcile it.
>
> As I explored and asked questions, I realized that all 3 of those ways to reconcile it were flawed once you gave them closer scrutiny. For me, the concept of Hell was the first crack in the armor of my belief.
>
> I think it's the reason that in a lot of places "torment in Hell" has been replaced by "absence of God". Now that the world is smaller, it's not unknown people in strange places that are going to Hell, it's that nice Somali lady who checks you out at the grocery store. We all feel a little better if instead of being tortured by Satan, she is merely ... gone.

---

[1] "How can finite transgressions deserve infinite punishment?", *Reddit*, https://www.reddit.com/r/DebateReligion/comments/7ujtg4/how_can_finite_transgressions_deserve_infinite/ (accessed 02/11/2021).

I have actually come across examples of pulling at the frayed thread of hell being the beginning of the eventual unravelling of the whole suite of theistic beliefs. I found this when collecting accounts of deconversion for a previous book, *Beyond an Absence of Faith*. Satan and hell are so deeply problematic that the merest of scrutiny leaves the ideas crumbling before you, and the whole religious worldview can follow close behind.

Hell is not a nice idea. And the sooner the idea of hell is put to bed, the mentally healthier people will be. Indeed, research has shown that "belief in Hell is associated with lower happiness and life satisfaction at the national…and individual…level".[1]

It makes no sense, it offers no value in and of itself, it offers little value to society as an idea, so why the hell is it still conceptually hanging around?

The answer, I think, is that certain people can't get away from the intuitive pull of retribution. "You're not like me, you've done some serious wrongs, you've rejected my belief system and therefore rejected me, so you're going to pay for it. For a long, long time."

Surely we can outgrow this sort of belief system by taking on broad understanding and compassion. After all, it might even be something Jesus would do…

[1] Shariff, Azim and Aknin, Lara, "The Emotional Toll of Hell: Cross-National and Experimental Evidence for the Negative Well-Being Effects of Hell Beliefs", *PLoS*, https://journals.plos.org/plosone/article?id=10.1371/journal.pone.0085251 (accessed 02/11/2021).

Part Six

OTHER INCOHERENT IDEAS

We have had a little romp through some of the long grasses of theology, and we are still left with a few persistent ideas clinging on for dear life.

One of the main areas left to dip into is the world of prayer. Prayer is a concept that has similar characteristics to the soul. It is somewhat nebulous and ingrained into our popular psyche, but when you unpick it a little, it looks rather more incoherent than you previously thought.

We have seen how difficult it is to reconcile the traits of OmniGod with the world we see around us. We have also explored how those traits are internally inconsistent and incompatible. Now we can think about what it would be like to communicate with that being and for the being to act upon our demands and desires, our innermost worries and confessions. Keep in mind that it had designed and created the world to be in that way anyway, and would already know our demands and desires, those innermost worries and confessions. It would already know how much we would praise and worship it before we heaped praise and worship on it.

"Here it comes, here it comes… Aaah, let that praise wash over me, let those songs delight me, fill my nostrils with the holy smell of burnt offerings and charred animal flesh!"

Who says God lacks nothing, and has no desires or needs? Oh, yes, it's ontologically perfect. Sorry, I'd forgotten that.

28 – Prayer Makes Little Sense

There are, admittedly, many different reasons for praying. Some have more coherent rationale behind them than others. The main reasons include the following:

- Adoration, praise, worship.
- Confession.
- Thanksgiving.
- Petition, supplication (asking for stuff), intercession (asking God for help on behalf of oneself or others).

I will deal with the last two first because they make the least sense.

OmniGod knows the future and cannot act contrary to its own infallible predictions and beliefs about how the world will be. In other words, there is no way that the world can change the way it will develop, and this is due to God's infallible foreknowledge.

God is omniscient. It has thought of all counterfactuals and all possible ramifications of all possible scenarios. Therefore, praying to God to ask it for something – more money, a team to win, a special favour, an intervention of some sort, and so on – is completely and utterly *pointless* as far as the desired outcome is concerned.

The following isn't what will ever happen:

Praying believer: "Dear God, please help me to get this job [score this point, end world hunger, win the lottery, find a partner, etc.].

Please. I beg you. It will help my family and allow me to keep my house."

God: "Ah, that's a really good idea. I hadn't thought about you getting that job. I had planned otherwise, but I now realise that your desire and reasoning, mere mortal, are actually better than my plan! I'm so stupid, I never saw it! Here you go."

There is no way we will ever change OmniGod's mind. It supposedly happened a few times in the Bible, except it didn't. Those stories (at Nineveh, for example) are mythological and involve an iteration of God that is less sophisticated than in the modern day. God won't change its mind concerning creation just because you have asked it to, not least because it invalidates its own omniscience.

So intercession and petition are non-starters. They are not even remotely coherent ideas here.

God also knows the hearts and minds of all of its creations. There is no need to get people to confess at all, since God already knows. Knows what we have done, and knew our deviations before we deviated.

God also knows how thankful we are without having to thank it. And, as such, God already knows how much you appreciate it. Worse still, it is rather narcissistic of God to create all of these entities, these minions, that it expects to routinely publicly adore and worship it (not to mention make burnt offering animal sacrifices as we see in the Hebrew Bible!). Are we merely instruments in God's own personal psychological self-aggrandisement?

The only thing that is left is in the actual act of praying – that praying gives some kind of mental advantage or improvement. Whilst God knows in advance what you are praying for, and so the prayer conveys literally nothing of use to God, it builds up your spiritual muscles, exercising your soul.

Or some such thing.

This is all that's left for the theist. And, yes, just like homeopathy, there might be a useful placebo effect for some. Mental wellbeing can also be achieved by meditation as well, for example. Then again, perhaps the activity of prayer does improve some relationship dynamics between the believer praying and God.

What we are left with, though, is a really esoteric understanding of prayer that is far removed from why we are told to do it and what the holy books say of prayer.

Or, prayer makes very little sense indeed.

29 – Prayer Is Not Effective

Some (but not an awful lot of) research has been carried out into the efficacy of prayer. I say not an awful lot because it is, considering the number of people in the world who do it, the most common form of complementary "medicine" that is used. Throughout the world and over time, prayer has been used on an enormous scale.

Of course, I feel dirty using the word "prayer" in terms of "medicine".

Before I stun you with the overwhelmingly contradictory and problematic research into the efficacy of prayer, it is worth noting that the wrong type of research is carried out. What I mean by this is that people only test how effective prayer is in making people better from routine naturalistic operations or conditions. For example, a study into how well people fare after heart surgery will look at different variables, to see if someone who was prayed for recovered better or quicker than someone who wasn't.

But no study has looked at how effective prayer is at regrowing limbs. Or bringing people back to life.

Because, of course, it isn't. Effective. At all. Ever.

So the only effectiveness that prayer can realistically obtain is in making someone *feel* they are being helped and looked after by God so that they might somehow put mind over matter. A better mental wellbeing could then cause a physical placebo effect. The whole process is just an amelioration of a natural scenario.

It could be, of course, that God decides to *only* help people who could recover naturally from a given situation.

But, in reality, this looks like God doesn't exist because limbs don't regrow and people don't come back to life.

First-person studies – ones that look at how prayer affects the person praying – are inconclusive. Part of the problem seems to be issues with self-reporting in such studies. Prayer may actually reduce stress or anxiety (thus increasing wellbeing). Or the people reporting on these studies might well *want* prayer to have this effect, so they report it as *having* this effect. This is known as *self-report* bias. There are various sorts of subjective biases with such first-person research. And, as mentioned, less prayerful things like meditation and yoga can also deliver similar outcomes.

One interesting study of prayer in British secondary (high) schools on students does have data worth reporting here. In "Prayer and psychological health: A study among sixth-form pupils attending Catholic and Protestant schools in Northern Ireland", the authors found that:[1]

> Among pupils attending both Catholic and Protestant schools higher levels of prayer were associated with lower psychoticism scores. Among pupils attending Catholic schools, however, higher levels of prayer were also associated with higher neuroticism scores.

Make of that what you will.

Third-party studies are more interesting. Researchers in these studies secure more objective data from individuals using external benchmarks and consistent metrics. Objective clinical studies into the effects of prayer need to be rigidly carried out and methodologically sound, using double-blind protocols and randomisation. In such studies, neither the patient nor the doctor knows whether they got the real drug or the placebo (prayer or no prayer). And it is apportioned

[1] Francis et al (2008), "Prayer and psychological health: A study among sixth-form pupils attending Catholic and Protestant schools in Northern Ireland", *The University of Warwick*, https://wrap.warwick.ac.uk/2894/1/WRAP_Francis_0673558-ie-170210-prayer_and_psychological_health.pdf (accessed 02/11/2021).

randomly. Procedures such as these eliminate many of the biases that other studies can be prone to.

Unfortunately, a good number of prayer studies have been either poorly designed, methodologically flawed or even downright fraudulent. Of the well-conducted experiments, results have consistently showed that prayer has a statistical "null" effect.

One of the most comprehensive pieces of research, "Study of the Therapeutic Effects of Intercessory Prayer (STEP)",[1] tested the effectiveness of prayer on roughly 1800 patients undergoing coronary artery bypass surgery. Of the groups, the group not receiving prayer had 51% complication or mortality rate, the prayer group had 52%, and the group that knew they were being prayed for had a 59% complication or mortality rate! It seems that knowing about being prayed for can give you the jitters when preparing for major surgery.

There are simply not enough decent, rigorous studies with replicated results to have any kind of robust conclusion that prayer works. And even then, it only works as a placebo effect to help people naturalistically recover.

Here are three examples from different metadata analyses:

- 2003: This analysis reported some benefit from prayer, but admitted that of all the studies, "only three have sufficient rigor for review here" and that in all three, "the strongest findings were for the variables that were evaluated most subjectively".[2] In other words, there was a subjectivity bias.

- 2006: The analysis concluded that, of 14 studies, there is "no discernible effect".[3]

---

[1] Benson, H. et al. (2006), "Study of the Therapeutic Effects of Intercessory Prayer (STEP) in cardiac bypass patients: a multicenter randomized trial of uncertainty and certainty of receiving intercessory prayer", *American Heart Journal* 151 (4): p. 934–42.
[2] Powell L.H. et al (2003). "Religion and spirituality. Linkages to physical health", *The American Psychologist,* 58 (1): p. 36–52.
[3] Masters, K. et al, (2006), "Are there demonstrable effects of distant intercessory prayer? A meta-analytic review", *Annals of Behavioral Medicine,* 32 (1): p. 21–6.

- 2007: A review of intercessory prayer produced inconclusive results, noting that the three most rigorous studies "failed to produce significant findings", stating of the whole analysis that "[t]he findings are unlikely to satisfy either proponents or opponents of intercessory prayer."[1]

My conclusion? Prayer is not only nonsensical, but also not effective.

---

[1] Hodge, David R. (2007), "A Systematic Review of the Empirical Literature on Intercessory Prayer", *Research on Social Work Practice,* 17 (2): p. 174–187.

30 – But God Is Not OmniGod According to the Bible

Yes, this will be a Bible-centric argument. I thought I would (almost) finish the book off with an observation or two made in the Bible itself. God is not, in fact, omniscient; nor is it omnipotent; nor, as we have seen in an earlier argument or two, is it omnibenevolent.

It's time for a whirlwind trip around the Bible, focusing on whether God does indeed know everything and is indeed all-powerful.

One of the problems with the Bible is that it is contradictory. This is largely because it is not one book but a collection of books written and compiled over time, with different authors wrangling in different contexts with what God actually is or was (to them).

For example, the Hebrew Bible was written in different times and places by different people. The authors incorporated a range of oral traditions. And then different editors using these multiple sources redacted the stories into something meaningful...to them. This is why some stories or parts of stories are repeated as many as four times within the text, why outright contradictions exist, why discontinuity exists, and why redundancy through repetition exists. *All of this* is explained by multiple sources. However, literalists struggle to give a coherent explanation of each and every issue with the collection, littering the text with individual sticking plaster fixes until it is weighed down by its own solutions to its own lack of coherence.

This then evolved from the Hebrew Bible to the Christian Bible as the New Testament was added by those who believed a chap from ~~Nazareth Bethlehem~~ Nazareth was ~~the Messiah~~ God. All of these claims about God came from different places and from authors with different agendas. For example, I argue that the authors of the Synoptic Gospels (Mark, Matthew, and Luke, or not, as the case may be) did not believe Jesus was God, but was the Messiah – a Jewish divinely exalted figure. That Jesus was actually *God* in human form was a later evolution of thinking, starting with the Gospel of John (John 1):

> **1** In the beginning was the Word, and the Word was with God, and the Word was God. **2** He was in the beginning with God. **3** All things came into being through Him, and apart from Him not even one thing came into being that has come into being. **4** In Him was life, and the life was the Light of mankind. **5** And the Light shines in the darkness, and the darkness did not grasp it.

This was a big theological step away from the previous Gospel writers. But people today seek to read the Christian Bible *as one coherent text* with *one voice*. It is not.

As a result, we get a mishmash of ideas struggling to provide clarity and coherence.

The Bible claims multiple times throughout that God is all-powerful: Matthew 19:26; Psalm 147:5; Luke 1:37; Jeremiah 32:17; Job 42:2; and so on. But the Bible also claims that there are some things God cannot do.

In Judges 1:19 we are told almighty God is unable to defeat the Judahites' enemies because they had iron chariots:

> Now the Lord was with Judah, and they took possession of the hill country; but they could not drive out the inhabitants of the valley, because they had iron chariots.

Well this seems a little…weak.

The Tower of Babel is another biblical story that, when read literally (as many theists are inclined to do) shows God to be somewhat less than it should be.

In Genesis 11, humans, full of pride and ambition, get together to build a tower whose top could reach up to heaven. In seeing this (already we have the idea that God is not omniscient because it should have already known what was going to happen), God believes that humans could become omnipotent (Genesis 11:6). As a result, it afflicts them with so many languages that humans are unable to understand each other. This causes them to scatter across the Earth.

Of course, this is an aetiological story designed to explain certain phenomena – languages and the distribution of people. But if you are a biblical literalist, this story poses a few problems (e.g., that we now regularly build towers much higher than the one in Babel, and we have even been to the moon…).

Here are some verses that also show that God cannot do certain things (change, lie, etc.). I previously pointed out in earlier arguments how God's characteristics constrain what it is truly able to do:

> … there is no variation or shifting shadow … (James 1:17).

> …the fact that His purpose is unchangeable… (Hebrews 6:17)

> It is impossible for God to lie. (Hebrews 6:18)

> …in the hope of eternal life, which God, who cannot lie, promised long ages ago… (Titus 1:2)

> God cannot be tempted by evil, and He Himself does not tempt anyone. (James 1:13)

> If we are faithless, He remains faithful, for He cannot deny Himself. (2 Timothy 2:13)

Where the Bible struggles even more is with omniscience – knowing and seeing all things.

Famously, God can't find Adam and Eve (Genesis 3:8-9):

> [8] Now they heard the sound of the Lord God walking in the garden in the cool of the day, and the man and his wife hid themselves from the presence of the Lord God among the trees of the garden. [9] Then the Lord God called to the man, and said to him, "Where are you?"

There are many more examples, including the following: Cain was able to be hidden from God (Genesis 4:14-16); God didn't know where Sarah was (Genesis 18:1-9); when God was about to murder everyone in Sodom and Gomorrah, it wondered "Shall I hide from Abraham what I am about to do", thus indicating it didn't know its future actions; God didn't know that Abraham feared it (Genesis 22:12); God didn't know who it was wrestling with (Genesis 32:27-30); it didn't know who was with Balaam (Numbers 22:9); it didn't know what was in the Israelites hearts for forty years (Deuteronomy 8:2) despite knowing what is in everyone's hearts (Psalm 44:21; Acts 1:24); it didn't know whether the Israelites would obey it or not (Judges 2:22)... I could go on.

The biblical theist could argue that the Bible is written by people who, though inspired, are writing symbolically and allegorically. This obviously invalidates literalism but also throws into question exactly what we then know to be *true* in the Bible. How do we know what is allegory, symbolism, allusion, and...fact?

That said, there are many *other* reasons to disbelieve the Bible: history archaeology, nonsensical theology, anthropology, philosophy, etc. For some of these approaches, please see some of my other books (*The Nativity: A Critical Examination*; *The Resurrection: A Critical Examination of the Easter Story*; *Not Seeing God*; and *Why I am Atheist and Not a Theist*).

The final story here that shows that God really doesn't have omniscience is Noah's flood story. This never happened. However, the majority of theists think that it did in pretty much the same way the Bible describes it:[1]

> BIBLE STORIES - Overall, 64 percent believe the story of Moses parting the Red Sea is "literally true, meaning it happened that way word-for-word." About as many say the same about creation (61 percent) and Noah and the flood (60 percent). About three in 10 say, instead, that each of these is "meant as a lesson, but not to be taken literally."
>
> There is wide variation in the numbers of literal readers across groups, but much of it is driven by two factors - religious belief and frequency of practice.
>
> Literal belief peaks among evangelical Protestants, and especially among evangelical Protestants who attend church at least once a week. In that group, 96 percent take the Red Sea story literally. It's a still-high 85 percent among evangelical Protestants who attend church less often.

The background to the story is important (forgetting that it was appropriated from pre-existing myths in neighbouring cultures). As Genesis 6 explains:

> [5] Then the Lord saw that the wickedness of mankind was great on the earth, and that every intent of the thoughts of their hearts was only evil continually. [6] So the Lord was sorry that He had made mankind on the earth, and He was grieved in His heart. [7] Then the Lord said, "I will wipe out mankind whom I have created from the face of the land; mankind, and animals as well, and crawling things, and the birds of the sky. For I am sorry that I have made them." [8] But Noah found favor in the eyes of the Lord.

---

[1] See the 2003 poll "Six in 10 Take Bible Stories Literally, But Don't Blame Jews for Death of Jesus", *ABC News*, https://abcnews.go.com/images/pdf/947a1Viewsof theBible.pdf (accessed 11/11/2021).

We must understand that this is a story of God killing all of humanity, bar eight. And all of the animal kingdom bar two of each kind (or seven depending on which iteration of the story from Genesis you read). That is an awful lot of death. Why? Because God *then* realised how wicked humanity had become. It either never knew this before or it is very forgetful.

In fact, the whole nature of the story is one big invalidation of its omni-characteristics. God realises that it has messed up in that its designed and created humans were all wicked, destroys them all and starts over, all the while promising never to send such floods and destruction again. This is a very human – anthropomorphic – god acting in a very human, non-omniscient way.

God is clearly showing a limited knowledge of how its creation would operate going forward – it is being reactive and not proactive. Simply put, this story as told invalidates God's omniscience and foreknowledge.

A truly omnibenevolent and omniscient god would not have knowingly designed and created something for the main components to go wrong at the start and then have to destroy them all (you know, with healthy loving dollops of suffering and death) and start again. This is incompetence at best, and malevolence at worst.

Or, the flood never happened and OmniGod doesn't exist.

There, fixed it.

Bonus Argument: God Is Not Omniscient Because It Could Be Living in *The Matrix*

Okay, let's add one for fun. A bit of philosophical last-orders-at-the-bar time. I think we've got time to squeeze this last one in.

The film *The Matrix* is an incarnation of philosopher René Descartes' Evil Daemon thought experiment (as it was later coined). The idea was to work out what we know to be indubitably true and build up our epistemological framework (theories of knowledge) from there. He concluded, using *cogito ergo sum* (I think; therefore, I am) that we can be certain – really, truly certain – of only *one* thing: we go about our day by thinking, experiencing, and doubting. And whatever it is that is doing the thinking, experiencing and doubting, exists.

Everything else could be a dream. Or it could be that an evil daemon is putting sensations into our head. Or we are a brain in a vat, or that we are living in *The Matrix*, with our bodies plugged into experience machines.

I don't want to thrash out all of the philosophy involved in this, but the end result is that we can't *prove* that we aren't any of those things – a dream, the work of a daemon, a brain in a vat, or a character in *The Matrix*. We can't indubitably *know* that we aren't. And, yes, this does depend how you define "know" (does knowledge have to be indubitable?). But for the purposes of this piece, let's assume a theistic layperson's understanding of the term such that God knowing something is having knowledge of all true propositions.

Interestingly, it is as a result of arguments like this that modern Christian philosophers are starting to see that a more coherent version

183

of omniscience might be a *limited maximal knowledge.* This process is a gradual chipping away of God's properties so that God moves from the "being than which no greater can be conceived" down to some kind of degraded feasibility.[1]

Anyway, we can't prove that we are not living in *The Matrix* or not a brain in a vat having stimuli inputted directly into our brains and minds. We carry on regardless, since it appears to make no discernible difference to our lives. We don't *think* we are living in such a way, but hey ho, we've got money to earn and food to buy for our families.

Likewise, God.

No, it doesn't need to buy food for its family, but this argument is just as applicable to God.

God also cannot indubitably *know* that its own mind is not victim to such a scenario. It may *think* it is a necessary god. It may even *be* a necessary god. But it can't *know* it is a necessary god.

It could be that there is another god in an ontological layer above the first god. And perhaps (or perhaps not) another above that god. In fact, it could be turtles all the way up. There could be an infinite trail of gods leading up from the first god, and *none* of those gods would know if it was the one necessary god that started the chain, though any of them *could* be.

This arguably invalidates the claim that God is omniscient.

And I think that's a suitably head-scratchy moment to end these arguments.

---

[1] A good place to start in seeing the compromises that might have to be made is in Wierenga, Edward (2021), "Omniscience", *Stanford Encyclopedia of Philosophy*, https://plato.stanford.edu/entries/omniscience (accessed 03/11/2021).

Conclusion

WHERE DOES THIS LEAVE THE THEIST?

OmniGod is a collection of properties and characteristics that just don't get on well with each other, fighting like ferrets in a bag.

Personally, I think it is about time that humanity outgrew these childish ideas. We've got bigger problems to solve – local problems, societal problems, national problems, global problems. These major or existential challenges that humanity faces are made all the more difficult by persistent beliefs in an outdated idea that promotes people to coalesce in ~~tribes~~ churches and religious communities to divide and fragment society. Such a fractured world is a severe hindrance to getting stuff done, to finding solutions.

A book like this may look like mental masturbation in terms of playing with abstract ideas and scratching one's head over this or that potential or this or that hypothetical, but it can and should have real-world consequences. Eventually, the tide will be unstoppable, and King Canute[1] will have to submit to the way the world is, not the way he thinks it is. Christianity, Islam, Judaism – theism in general – are in an intellectually perilous position. The secular tide has turned and it is coming in, where it should stay. Okay, analogies have been sufficiently stretched.

---

[1] A story from the Middle Ages where King Canute demonstrates to his flattering courtiers that he has no control over the incoming tide, explaining that secular power is vain compared to the supreme power of God.

Yet, humans are funny things, and we end up being far more psychological than rational. Cognitive dissonance trumps a good logical syllogism.

This book is both ammunition for those fighting the good fight and fodder for those doubting the good doubt. At some point, the conspiracy falls apart. At some point, the denier has to admit that the moon landing really did happen.

At least, I hope they do.

This project should leave the theist in no doubt that OmniGod does not exist. Does this mean that God does not exist? No. Yet this collection should really present itself as the thread that the theist knows they should not pull because the comfort blanket will quickly unravel. But that they can't help but pull anyway. A lesser god is surely a less satisfying god, and certainly not the god presented in the Bible or Qu'ran. That said, many different gods are presented in the Bible: Yahweh, Jesus, the Holy Spirit, omniscient but not quite knowing everything, omnipotent but not quite being able to do everything, omnibenevolent but actually malevolent…

God.

A small word but a big idea. An idea that, at the end of the day, just doesn't work very well.

Where then? Well, I often claim that (belief in) God is functional. When we start understanding the function of such a belief – existential comfort, plugging a lack of understanding or knowledge, certainty in a world of unknowns, balancing the books, and so on – then we can start working out whether to replace those ideas with more accurate and apt secular ones based in reality, or to wash those ideas away wholesale.

Atheists might not be able to comfort someone with promissory notes of eternity in heaven, so we can't replace that with an equivalent atheistic comforting appeal to some perfect afterlife. So we wash that idea away and talk about making the most of this life here.

On the other hand, we can replace God's explanatory power with the scientific method, the huge and growing body of knowledge about how the universe works. But we also shouldn't be afraid to say, "I don't know (but I have pretty good reason to think we will find out)."

For me, I am pretty certain that God does not exist. So it's up to me – it's up to us – to build everything from the ground up, not from the sky down. We achieve more when we build together and towards common goals, working to the same blueprints.

That said, sometimes we have to tear old rickety buildings down before we build new, sturdier, more sustainable ones. I am not deluded enough to think that this book is a swing of a wrecking ball, but more a blow of a sledgehammer. No, it's not the mythological fun of the supernaturally feather-light Mjölnir, but the rational importance of an enlightenment hammer, breaking holes in the dark walls to allow the brightness of the world to shine through.

Let's work with the rays of reality to build something new, something better.